Year 4 Contents

To the student

We write to express our thoughts, feelings, opinions and experiences; and to communicate with others. We might write stories, emails, diaries, greetings, lists, poems, reports, personal recounts, and much more.

When we write, we need to construct sentences that make sense and sound right, and spell our words correctly, so that others can understand what we mean.

This book will help you to become 'spelling wise' and 'writing ready'. Spelling is very closely linked to grammar (the way we put our sentences together).

In this book, you will learn how words look and sound and how to use these words correctly in your writing. When we write, we are constantly adding endings to words, so that what we write sounds right and makes sense. This book contains tips and spelling rules to help you become a great speller. Check out the Top 3 rules on the back page!

Common endings: -s, -es, -ing, -ed, -y, -er, -est and -ly.

About the author

Del has enjoyed a long career in education as a specialist teacher (Learning Difficulties), education adviser and regional coordinator (English). She has written extensively for parents, teachers and students and is a well-known and respected author nationally and internationally. Her publications cover a diverse range of print and electronic materials in English grammar, spelling, reading, writing and comprehension. She is the author of the popular *Reading Quest* books, a series of readers written for the older, reluctant reader.

Among her latest works are *Blake's Guide to Comprehension*, *Blake's Grammar Guide for primary students* and *Targeting Grammar*.

How to Use This Book

Your *Targeting Spelling Activity Book* is set out in units.
Each unit contains two word lists.

SEE & SAY

crust
plump
junk
bunch

SEE & SAY

The words in this list target a particular spelling skill. Look at these words and say them aloud several times. Say the last sound in each word loudly. This will help you to remember what the whole word looks like, and what it sounds like. The *See and Say* words provide a warm-up for the activities that follow.

I
am
the

LOOK & LEARN

These words are used all the time in writing to hold ideas together. They often never change their spelling, no matter where you place them in a text. Learn these words with your eyes, like this:

1. Write the word in large letters on a piece of paper or a whiteboard.
2. Look at the word and say it three times.
3. Close your eyes and picture the word.
4. Open your eyes and check. Is the word the same as your picture?
5. Close your eyes and picture the word again. Write it in the air with your finger.
6. Check. Is that the word you wrote?
7. Now, cover the word and write it again from your memory.
8. Check. If the word is not correct, go back to Step 2 and try again.

MEMORY TRAINING

Spelling is a skill that requires you to remember the words you want to write. When you see this sign, go back to a previous *See and Say* list and say the words two or three times, focusing on what they look and sound like. Then write as many words as you can remember. Soon, they will start to roll off the end of your pencil!

The more you write, the better your spelling will be.

Short Vowels

Short vowels have a short, snappy sound.

a	e	i	o	u

SEE & SAY

a	e	i	o	u
drag	smell	skip	drop	crust
grab	step	thick	lock	plump
crack	mend	pinch	frost	junk
splash	stretch	blink	strong	bunch

1 Name the pictures. *(Hint: All contain short vowels)*

When there is only *one* consonant after a short vowel, **double** that consonant before adding **-ing** or **-ed**. *Examples: run, **running**; hop, **hopped***
If there are already *two* consonants after a short vowel, just add an ending.
*Examples: jump, **jumped**; pack, **packing***

2 Complete this table of present and past tense verbs.

Add -ing		Add -ed	
smell	______	drag	______
grab	______	crack	______
lock	______	skip	______
blink	______	stretch	______
step	______	drop	______

LOOK & LEARN

children
often
want
their

TARGETING SPELLING 4 © PASCAL PRESS ISBN 9781925490220

UNIT 1

3 Add endings to the words in bold to complete the sentences correctly.

That morning, the fog became **thick**____ and the wind became **strong**____.

I bought two **bunch**____ of bananas and some **crust**____ bread.

Jon **splash**____ into the waves and swam **strong**____ to the rocks.

The children are **run**______ and **skip**______ across the oval.

Because it was cold and **frost**____, I put on my **thick**______ coat.

4 Complete this table of rhyming words.

him	pump	lock
r______	l______	m______
d______	cl______	d______
gr______	d______	sh______
sw______	h______	st______
br______	st______	fl______
tr______	sl______	bl______

MEMORY TRAINING

Read the words in each list two times. How many words can you remember? Write them in your notebook. Check and write your scores here.

....

5 Match the words to their meanings.

trendy	a large piece of cloth used as a bed covering (noun)
trinket	a long curly strand of hair (noun)
scatter	modern; of the latest fashion (adjective)
ringlet	to throw all over the place (verb)
scamper	a small ornament such as a piece of jewellery (noun)
blanket	to run or hurry away quickly (verb)

Irregular verbs have a special past tense form. *Examples: come, came; tell, told; do, did.*

6 Write the special past tense forms of these verbs.

swim	______________	run	______________
send	______________	ring	______________
fall	______________	get	______________
go	______________	sit	______________
sing	______________	has	______________

7 Write sentences using the words champion and trumpet.

____

____

Long Vowels

Long vowels have the same **name** and **sound**. Words containing a long vowel often end in a **silent e**. *Examples: cake, kite, rose, tube*

SEE & SAY

brake	fire	chose	amuse
scrape	tide	globe	accuse
safe	spice	stroke	refuse
whale	whine	erode	confuse
trade	shine	explode	excuse

Change the letter in bold to make two new words.

stone	place	made	tile	same	rode
stove	______	______	______	______	______
stole	______	______	______	______	______

When **verbs** end in **e**, drop the **e** before adding **-ing** and **-ed**.
*Examples: shake, shak**ing**; close, clos**ed***
Irregular verbs have a special past tense form.
Examples: wake, woke; come, came

Complete this table of present and past tense verbs.

take	taking	took	hope	______	______
scrape	______	______	ride	______	______
shine	______	______	explode	______	______
make	______	______	shake	______	______
amuse	______	______	race	______	______
trade	______	______	slide	______	______

Complete this table of rhyming words.

take		ice	
m______	r______	n______	sl______
c______	sh______	r______	sp______
l______	sn______	m______	tw______
f______	qu______	d______	pr______
fl______	br______	l______	adv______

MEMORY TRAINING

Read the words in each list two times. How many words can you remember? Write them in your notebook. Check and write your scores here.

....

TARGETING SPELLING 4 © PASCAL PRESS ISBN 9781925490220

push put sort strange

When words end in **e**, drop the **e** before adding **-y**. *Example: shake, shaky.*
Do **not** drop the **e** before adding **-ly**. *Examples: late, lately; rude, rudely*

4 Add -y or -ly to build adjectives or adverbs.

Add -y to build adjectives				Add -ly to build adverbs			
spice	______	rose	______	nice	______	safe	______
stone	______	taste	______	game	______	wise	______
lace	______	slime	______	grave	______	fine	______
shade	______	smoke	______	close	______	time	______
shine	______	race	______	late	______	brave	______

5 Write sentences to show how the words place and taste can be used 1. as a noun and 2. as a verb.

1 ______________________

2 ______________________

1 ______________________

2 ______________________

6 Join the word parts to make compound words.

rose	vine	snake	shake
fire	ship	cheese	away
grape	place	earth	skin
face	buds	milk	cake
space	book	take	quake

7 Join the syllables to read the words. Long vowels are marked like this: ō. Match the words and meanings. Use a dictionary to help you.

ex plō sion	relating to the whole world
con fū sion	the slow wearing away by wind or water
ē rō sion	a loud outburst
tī dal	coming at the end; last
glō bal	state of being muddled or mixed up
fīn al	relating to high and low tides

Long vowels say their own name!

The sound of ā

The sound of **ā** is represented by the letter teams **ai**, **ay**, and **ei** and the **final e** pattern **a _ e**. *Examples: sail, day, rein, gate*

SEE & SAY

plane	raise	display	weigh
mane	explain	relay	sleigh
tale	complain	delay	rein
wade	contain	decay	reign
grate	obtain	betray	eight

1 **Add endings to the words in bold to complete the sentences.**

The children **display**_____ the paper **plane**_____ they had made.

This **contain**_____ of cherries **weigh**_____ 500 **gram**_____.

We are **make**_____ sandcastles and they are **wade**_____ in the rock pools.

All **train**_____ and **bus**_____ were **delay**_____ by rain and local **flood**_____.

Molly is **grate**_____ carrots and I'm **chop**_____ the onions **fine**_____.

LOOK & LEARN

does done odd even

2 **Choose the correct do verb. Choose from do, does, did or done.**

__________ you know what Tyson __________ on Sundays?

I __________ my homework, but Terry has not __________ his.

Pam __________ not like bananas, but I __________.

__________ you all see what the mice have __________?

We __________ not want to go riding today, but Ellie __________.

Homophones are words that sound the same, but have different spelling.
Examples: see, sea; saw, sore; pain, pane

3 **Colour the correct homophone in each bracket.**

The creature had [pail pale] eyes and a very long [tail tale].

I bought a model [plain plane] at the toy [sail sale] last week.

The king's [rain reign] lasted for [ate eight] years.

The bus driver [maid made] a left turn into the [main mane] street.

The men will [way weigh] each [bail bale] of wool carefully.

TARGETING SPELLING 4 © PASCAL PRESS ISBN 9781925490220

Complete this table of rhyming words.

ate		rain	
m______	h______	m______	br______
l______	r______	p______	sl______
d______	gr______	tr______	st______
g______	sk______	gr______	str______

UNIT 3

MEMORY TRAINING

Read the words in each list two times. How many words can you remember? Write them in your notebook. Check and write your scores here.

....

Write the numbers between 1 and 10.

Synonyms are words that are similar in meaning.
Examples: flower / blossom; odd / strange; pretty / attractive / beautiful

Colour the pairs of words that are synonyms. Use a different colour for each pair.

decay	rule	contain	lift	stay	show	explain
tell	rot	display	reign	hold	raise	remain

Add the missing long vowels.

Milly will **gr__te** the carrots and I will **d__ce** the onions.

Oscar can **sk__te** across the **fr__zen** ice at great speed.

At the beach, we like to **w__de** through the **w__ves** as the **t__de** comes in.

The teacher explained how to **m__ke** a paper **pl__ne**.

Come over to my **pl__ce** for a **g__me** of cricket on Saturday.

Write the compound words.

day
- light ____________
- time ____________
- break ____________
- dream ____________
- bed ____________

play
- ground ____________
- pen ____________
- thing ____________
- room ____________
- time ____________

The sound of ē

The sound of **ē** is represented by the letter teams **ee** and **ea**. Included in this group are **eer** and **ear**. *Examples: **see**, **east**, **deer**, **fear***

SEE & SAY

agree	cease	near	cheer
degree	grease	fear	jeer
sneeze	season	gear	deer
squeeze	reason	clear	peer
coffee	creature	beard	steer

1 Add endings to the words in bold to complete the sentences.

squeeze Jan is ________________ oranges for their sweet juice.

grease The chef put the ________________ pan into hot, soapy water.

clear I can see ________________ with my new glasses.

reap The farmer is ________________ his summer wheat crop.

freeze Ice-cream is stored in the ________________ compartment.

2 Write the sea words.

sea
- shell ________________
- shore ________________
- weed ________________
- side ________________
- food ________________
- bed ________________

3 Add the missing letters to complete the compound words.

b _ _ hive	**s** _ _ **d** pod
t _ _ _ drops	**w** _ _ **k** end
p _ _ nuts	**tr** _ _ house
s _ _ **t** belt	**st** _ _ **m** boat
m _ _ **l** time	**wh** _ _ **l** chair
t _ _ pot	**b** _ _ keeper

4 Write words of opposite meaning and find them in the word search.

far ________________

late ________________

easy ________________

pull ________________

awake ________________

sour ________________

empty ________________

s	a	c	n	p	o
e	s	w	e	e	t
a	l	r	a	d	l
r	e	t	r	r	l
l	e	g	u	a	u
y	p	u	s	h	f

TARGETING SPELLING 4 © PASCAL PRESS ISBN 9781925490220

LOOK & LEARN

early around full pull

5 Add the missing letter teams. Choose from ee or ea.

Maddy will **p** __ __ **l** the potatoes for the evening **m** __ __ **l**.

This **w** __ __ **k**, apples and bananas are very **ch** __ __ **p**.

I took my rod and **r** __ __ **l** down to the **cr** __ __ **k** to fish.

We went to the game to **ch** __ __ **r** for our favourite **t** __ __ **m**.

Have you **b** __ __ **n** to see the **s** __ __ **ls** perform at Sea World?

I cut my **h** __ __ **l** on a piece of glass, but it will soon **h** __ __ **l**.

6 Colour the pairs of words that are synonyms. Use a different colour for each pair.

cease	reason	peer	animal	near	easy	steer
close	creature	stop	guide	simple	excuse	look

7 Join the syllables to read the words. Match the words to their meanings.

sea son ing — a signal showing the way or warning of danger (noun)

ref er ee — things that add flavour to food such as salt, herbs or spices (noun)

wea sel — person who gathers things washed up by the sea (noun)

bea con — cross; easily annoyed (adjective)

beach comb er — person who makes sure players follow the rules of a game (noun)

peev ish — a small animal that eats mice and rabbits (noun)

8 Write sentences to show how the words cheer and fear can be used 1. as a noun and 2. as a verb.

1 ______________________________

2 ______________________________

1 ______________________________

2 ______________________________

How many words can you remember?

Go back and choose any *See and Say* list. Read through it twice, focusing on how the words look and sound. Write as many words as you can remember in your notebook. Check how many you have written correctly and enter your score here.

The sound of ō

The sound of ō is represented by the letter teams **oa**, **ow** and the **final e** pattern **o _ e**. *Examples: boat, moan, show, yellow, rose, pole*

SEE & SAY

nose	rode	loaf	coast	borrow	elbow
close	wrote	load	throat	window	meadow
froze	whole	coax	approach	shadow	tomorrow

1 Write these nouns in plural form.

nose ____________ coast ____________ loaf ____________

crow ____________ bone ____________ elbow ____________

load ____________ meadow ____________ shadow ____________

2 Name the pictures. *(Hint: All are compound words)*

LOOK & LEARN

lose find poor only

3 Write the past tense of these irregular verbs.

Present tense	Past tense	Present tense	Past tense
ride	____________	write	____________
grow	____________	know	____________
drive	____________	make	____________
blow	____________	steal	____________
shake	____________	rise	____________

4 Add the missing letter teams. Choose from oa and ow.

Everywhere I go my dog **foll** _ _ **s** me like a **shad** _ _.

I didn't have a **rainc** _ _ **t**, so I got **s** _ _ **king** wet.

An archer shoots **arr** _ _ **s** from a **b** _ _.

Our **c** _ _ **ch** thinks our team will win **tomorr** _ _.

A **sh** _ _ **l** of fish is **appr** _ _ **ching** the south **c** _ _ **st**.

Antonyms are words that are opposite in meaning to each other.
Examples: hot / cold; wet / dry; old / young

5 Write antonyms for the underlined words.

If I lose my money, I may never ________________ it again.

Robin Hood robbed from the rich to give to the ________________.

I will ________________ the door and open the window.

We walked across a ________________ bridge over a wide river.

James is a fast runner, but I am rather ________________.

THE 'e' RULE

-y is often added to words to form **adjectives**. If the words end in **e**, drop the **e** before adding **-y**. *Examples: shine, shiny; smoke, smoky*

-ly is often added to words to form **adverbs**. If the words end in **e**, **do not** drop the **e** before adding **-ly**. *Examples: late, lately; wise, wisely*

6 Add -y or -ly to the word in bold to complete each sentence correctly.

rose Sheena has big blue eyes and ________________ red cheeks.

snow It was a cold and ________________ winter's day.

close Watch ________________. I will show you how to make a paper hat.

stone The horse galloped over the rough and ________________ ground.

slow A storm was ________________ approaching from the west.

lone If you are feeling ________________ come and play ball with me.

7 Complete this table of rhyming words.

mow		bone	
r______	bl______	l______	h______
b______	fl______	c______	st______
kn______	gr______	t______	dr______
sh______	cr______	ph______	thr______

MEMORY TRAINING

Read the words in each list two times. How many words can you remember? Write them in your notebook. Check and write your scores here.

....

8 Use the letters in this word to make new words.

coastline

Score 1 point for each 3-letter word.
Score 3 points for each 4-letter word.
Score 5 points for each 5-letter word.

3-letter words ____

4-letter words ____

____

5-letter words ____

The sound of ī

The sound of ī is represented by the letters i, ie, y, igh and the **final e** pattern i _ e. *Examples: kind, pie, my, high, bite*

SEE & SAY

bite	cry	pie	kind	fight
hike	dry	tie	blind	right
shine	fly	lie	wind	slight
life	fry	die	wild	might

1 Write these nouns in plural form. *(Note any rules)*

fight ______ life ______ pie ______
fly ______ knife ______ tie ______
cry ______ kite ______ lie ______

2 Add an ending to the word in bold to complete each sentence correctly.

hike The men are ______ through rugged bushland.

kind Bella is the ______ girl I know.

slight He left the door of his bedroom ______ open.

shine The dancers wore ______ red tap shoes.

mighty It is said that the pen is ______ than the sword.

3 Add the word light to complete these compound words.

sun ______ spot ______
day ______ head ______
moon ______ candle ______
bed ______ flash ______
lamp ______ foot ______

4 Write antonyms *(words of opposite meaning)*.

tame ______ day ______
dark ______ lose ______
black ______ left ______
wet ______ dull ______
narrow ______ nasty ______

LOOK & LEARN

who when why what where

TARGETING SPELLING 4 © PASCAL PRESS ISBN 9781925490220

The **wh-** words (**who**, **when**, **why**, **what** and **where**) are often used to ask questions. *Examples: **Why** were you late today? **Where** are you going? **When** is your birthday?*

5 Use a wh- word to ask these questions.

__________ did you go and __________ will you be back?

__________ is your name and __________ do you live?

__________ gave me this dollar and __________ will I buy with it?

__________ did you leave early and __________ did you go?

__________ are you building and __________ is helping you?

To change the tense of **regular verbs** ending in **y**, follow these simple rules:

1. Add **-ing** to all verbs ending in **y**. *Examples: play**ing**, carry**ing***
2. If the letter before the **y** is a vowel, just add **-s** or **-ed**.
   *Examples: play**s**, play**ed***
3. If the letter before the **y** is **not** a vowel, change **y** to **i** and add **-es** or **-ed**.
   *Examples: cr**y**, cr**ies**; cr**y**, cr**ied***

6 Complete the table of regular verbs showing verb tense.

cry	cries	crying	cried
dry			
fry			
try			
spy			

Note how to write the verb tense of verbs ending in ie, and complete the table.

tie	ties	tying	tied
lie			
die			

7 Complete this short quiz.

What do birds use their wings for? __________

What does the sun do? __________

What do you use to cut your food? __________

How many toes do you have on your left foot? __________

What word describes a person who cannot see? __________

What do bees live in? __________

What is the number after eight? __________

What is a bike used for? __________

Letter Teams: oo, ew

oo has two main sounds: the **oo** in *look* and the **oo** in *school*.
Other sounds are the **or** in *door* and the **uh** in *flood*.
ew also has an **oo** sound. *Examples: chew, flew*

SEE & SAY

				Odd Bods
wood	noon	chew	flood	group
good	soon	crew	blood	soup
hook	roof	screw	door	
shook	proof	knew	poor	
foot	tooth	jewel		

1 Write these nouns in their plural form. * *Care needed.*

foot* ________ goose* ________ hoof ________ group ________ tooth* ________ roof ________

2 Write the special past tense forms of these irregular verbs.

fly	flew	blow	________
shake	________	grow	________
know	________	choose	________
lose	________	take	________
throw	________	draw	________

3 Colour the pairs of words that make a compound word.
Use a different colour for each pair.

tooth	moon	school	screw	book	good
driver	mark	ache	bye	ground	light

4 Complete this table of rhyming words.

new		
d________	cr________	ch________
f________	gr________	kn________
fl________	dr________	st________
bl________	scr________	str________
br________	thr________	sp________

MEMORY TRAINING

Read the words in each list two times. How many words can you remember? Write them in your notebook. Check and write your score here.

....

TARGETING SPELLING 4 © PASCAL PRESS ISBN 9781925490220

LOOK & LEARN

can't don't isn't won't

5 Write a contraction for the words in bold.

Jason can play chess, but I **cannot**. ____________

I **do not** want to sing on stage by myself. ____________

Henry **is not** going to the football game on Saturday. ____________

Maddy **will not** be going to school today. ____________

The cows **are not** in the top paddock. ____________

6 Add the word foot to complete these compound words.

____________path	____________stool
____________ball	____________steps
____________bridge	____________prints
____________loose	____________lights

7 Write in the missing words.

Someone is knocking on my ____________.

The dentist filled a hole in my ____________.

I kicked the football into the goal with my left ____________.

Dad went up on the ____________ to clean out the gutters.

Timmy baited his ____________ and threw his line in the creek.

If the river breaks its bank, it will ____________ the city.

8 Find and fix the spelling mistakes. Write them on the lines.

I dont like mushroom soop. ____________ ____________

Sumone is knocking on the woodin door. ____________ ____________

Mr Potter new that the jewls were missing. ____________ ____________

This isnt the last groop of singers to perform. ____________ ____________

I cant cross the fludded river. ____________ ____________

9 Unscramble this list of Australian animals. Start with the letter in bold.

ssom**p**u	aao**k**l	ga**k**ronoa	**p**ysuplat	ancihd**e**
____________	____________	____________	____________	____________

Letter Teams: ou, ow

The letter team **ou** has an **ow** sound, as in *cloud* and *pouch*.
The letter team **ow** may also have this sound, as in *cow* and *clown*.

SEE & SAY

proud	found	bow	growl	an noun cer
cloud	sound	browse	howl	pro nounce
hour	mountain	down	eyebrow	sound less
flour	fountain	town	anyhow	sur round

Cross out (✗) the incorrect word in the brackets.

They waited for [hours ours] for the floodwaters to go [done down].

After the flood, there was the [fowl foul] smell of drying mud.

Place a cup of [flower flour] into a large mixing [bole bowl].

I will go to the nursery [know now] to buy a [flour flower] pot.

[Right Write] a note to your friend on this [peace piece] of paper.

Complete this table of rhyming words.

town	out	round
g_______	p_______	f_______
br_______	sp_______	s_______
cr_______	sc_______	h_______
cl_______	st_______	b_______
dr_______	sn_______	w_______
fr_______	sh_______	gr_______

MEMORY TRAINING

Read the words in each list two times. How many words can you remember? Write them in your notebook. Check and write your scores here.

....

LOOK & LEARN

somehow someone kept against

Write the down and out words.

down
- stairs _______________
- town _______________
- stream _______________
- wind _______________
- light _______________
- hill _______________

out
- doors _______________
- side _______________
- break _______________
- burst _______________
- line _______________
- skirts _______________

TARGETING SPELLING 4 © PASCAL PRESS ISBN 9781925490220

UNIT 8

4 Choose a word from the box to complete each sentence.

pronounce surrounded soundlessly announce mountainous

The city was ______________________ by floodwaters for several days.

It is fun to ______________________ the word, *supercalifragilisticexpialidocious*!

The male lion crept ______________________ towards its unsuspecting prey.

Our teacher will ______________________ the winner of the art competition.

The bushwalkers travelled through ______________________ country to the sea.

5 Add the missing letter teams. Choose from ou and ow.

A **cr** __ __ **d** of people gathered by the **f** __ __ **ntain** in the **t** __ __ **n** square.

I **f** __ __ **nd** the kitten **c** __ __ **ering** before a **gr** __ __ **ling** dog.

Today is **cl** __ __ **dy** and **sh** __ __ **ers** are expected in the coming **h** __ __ **rs**.

The baby kangaroo **b** __ __ **nded** into its mother's **p** __ __ **ch**.

Lost in the **m** __ __ **ntains**, the hikers **sh** __ __ **ted l** __ __ **dly** for help.

6 Write words of opposite meaning and find them in the word search.

up ______________

rich ______________

lost ______________

bad ______________

sweet ______________

open ______________

north ______________

dull ______________

soft* ______________

b	r	i	g	h	t	l
d	o	n	o	t	s	k
e	o	f	o	u	n	d
s	p	t	d	o	r	o
o	g	h	e	s	i	w
l	o	u	d	f	p	n
c	s	o	u	r	b	y

(of sound)

7 Join the syllables to read the words. Match the words to their meanings.

vow el	amazed; astonished; stunned (past participle)
cow ard	information told or made known to the public (noun)
bound ar y	one of 5 letters of the alphabet – a, e, i, o, u (noun)
a stound ed	the border, edge or limit of something (noun)
south ward	person eager to avoid danger, pain or difficulty (noun)
an nounce ment	moving towards the south (adverb)

How many words can you remember?

Go back and choose any *See and Say* list. Read through it twice, focusing on how the words look and sound. Write as many words as you can remember in your notebook. Check how many you have written correctly and enter your score here.

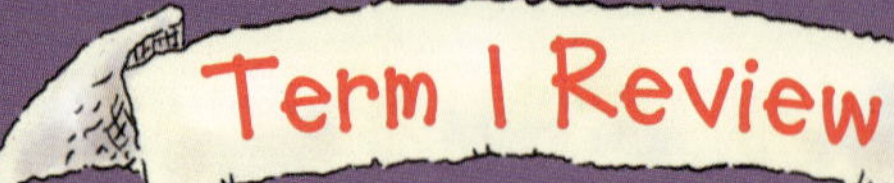

1 Name the pictures.

2 Write these nouns in plural form.

bunch	________	crack	________	tide	________
mouse	________	loaf	________	cry	________
life	________	group	________	leaf	________
foot	________	deer	________	tooth	________

3 Write the words of opposite meaning.

far	________	fat	________	hard	________
dangerous	________	late	________	sour	________
arrive	________	empty	________	fast	________
dirty	________	push	________	wet	________

4 Write the past tense of these irregular verbs.

ride	________	take	________	know	________
write	________	slide	________	shine	________
freeze	________	fly	________	shake	________
grow	________	choose	________	bite	________

5 Add the missing letters to complete the compound words.

p _ _ _ _ brush	**b** _ _ hive	**b** _ _ _ shelf	**m** _ _ _ _ trap
w _ _ _ _ barrow	**m** _ _ _ light	**r** _ _ _ bow	**r** _ _ _ _ about
p _ _ nuts	**f** _ _ _ ball	**u** _ _ _ _ ground	**s** _ _ _ flakes
c _ _ _ _ line	**g** _ _ _ _ vine	**w** _ _ _ end	**s** _ _ _ _ waves

TARGETING SPELLING 4 © PASCAL PRESS ISBN 9781925490220

6 Colour the correct word in the brackets.

We travelled along a dusty [rode road] beside a babbling [creak creek].

A [wail whale] is a [great grate] creature of the [see sea].

I [made maid] a [write right] hand turn into the [mane main] street.

I put [for four] cakes in a [plane plain] paper bag and [tide tied] it with ribbon.

[To Two] boys [ate eight] a [hole whole] pizza between them.

7 Add endings. *(Remember the rules)*

Add -ing (present participles)		Add -ed (past participles)		Add -er (to build nouns)	
drag	______	dry	______	win	______
skate	______	chew	______	stretch	______
die	______	drop	______	rub	______
step	______	refuse	______	swim	______

8 Add -y to build adjectives. *(Remember the rules.)*

smell	______	grease	______	nose	______
grub	______	shine	______	fun	______
spice	______	shake	______	sand	______
rose	______	skin	______	race	______

9 Write the missing letters. Choose from ee and ea.

We **p** _ _ **red** at the tiny **s** _ _ **cr** _ _ **tures** in the **cl** _ _ **r** blue water.

Autumn is the **s** _ _ **son** when **l** _ _ **ves** change colour and fall.

Mum **squ** _ _ **zed** the **sw** _ _ **t**, juicy oranges and I grated the **ch** _ _ **se**.

We could **h** _ _ **r** the crowd **ch** _ _ **ring** for their favourite **t** _ _ **ms**.

I found pretty **s** _ _ **shells** and **s** _ _ **w** _ _ **d** on the sandy **b** _ _ **ch**.

10 Circle the spelling mistakes. Write the correct words on the lines.

Six raindeer pulled the heavy wooden slay. ______ ______

I rose erly to go for a jog arund the lake. ______ ______

Tom cryed when he loosed his red balloon. ______ ______

Were are you going tomorra? ______ ______

Billy hasnt dun his homework yet. ______ ______

The sound of or

The sound of **or** can be written as **au** (*sauce*, *Paul*); **aw** (*saw*, *lawn*); **oar** (*roar*, *board*); and **ore** (*more*, *shore*).

SEE & SAY

				Odd Bods
pause	draw	roar	shore	talk
cause	drawer	soar	score	walk
caught	yawn	coarse	bore	stalk
taught	prawn	hoarse	adore	
applaud	awful	board	ignore	

1 Join a word in Column A and a word in Column B to write a compound word.

A	B	Compound word
lawn	mill	
jaw	board	
saw	mower	
score	bone	

A	B	Compound word
draw	flakes	
bush	line	
corn	walk	
shore	bridge	

2 Complete this table of rhyming words.

saw	born
j______	c______
p______	h______
l______	t______
r______	w______
cl______	sh______

MEMORY TRAINING

Read the words in each list two times. How many words can you remember? Write them in your notebook. Check and write your scores here.

....

THE 'e' RULE

When a word ends in **e**, drop the **e** before adding **-ing**. *Example: bore, boring*
Do **not** drop the **e** before adding **-ly**. *Example: sore, sorely*

3 Add an ending to the word in bold to complete each sentence correctly.

cause A cat ran across the street ________________ me to brake suddenly.

soar An eagle ________________ high above the mountain tops.

drawer My study desk has four ________________.

score I kicked the ball into the net ________________ the first goal.

coarse Chop the nuts ________________ and toss into the salad.

begin Tim read the sports magazine from ________________ to end.

TARGETING SPELLING 4 © PASCAL PRESS ISBN 9781925490220

LOOK & LEARN before beside begin because

4 Clap the syllables in these words. Write a syllable in each box. Write the number of the word beside its meaning. Use a dictionary to help you.

No.	Word	Syllable	Syllable	No.	Meaning
1	scornful				State of being tired or weary of something
2	tawdry				Not active as if asleep or resting
3	storage				Cheap, showy, gaudy
4	dormant				A place to keep things
5	boredom				Showing disgust or contempt

5 Cross out (✗) the incorrect word in the brackets.

Lions [raw roar] and eagles [saw soar].

The [stalk stork] has [caught court] a fish in the shallow water.

[Pour Paw] some water into the tub for your thirsty [hoarse horse].

There was a loud [roar raw] when the players went on [caught court].

The [horse hoarse] galloped around the race [coarse course].

6 Complete this table of irregular past tense verbs.

teach	______	see	______	shoot	______
draw	______	tear	______	blow	______
wear	______	fly	______	shine	______
know	______	shake	______	catch	______

7 Join the syllables to write these words. Discuss their meanings with a friend.

or bit	______	or chard	______
or phan	______	or chid	______
or nate	______	or der	______
or gan	______	or din ar y	______

8 Write sentences to show how the words walk and board can be used 1. as a noun and 2. as a verb.

1 ______________________________

2 ______________________________

1 ______________________________

2 ______________________________

Tricky Letter: a

The letter **a** can represent different sounds. *Examples: hat* (short sound); *hate* (long sound); *last* (**ar** sound); *wash* (**o** sound)

SEE & SAY

last	glass	halt	wand
past	task	salt	wander
half	mask	scald	wasp
calf	calm	wash	waltz
class	palm	squash	wallet

Add a to complete the words, then write them in their plural form.

c__lf ________________ w__sp ________________

gl__ss ________________ h__lf ________________

w__ltz ________________ cl__ss ________________

Complete these rhyming words.

ask	t______	m______	b______	fl______
past	f______	c______	m______	bl______
pass	cl______	gl______	gr______	br______

Don't confuse **passed** (verb) and **past** (preposition).
Passed is the past tense form of the verb, **pass**.
*Example: I **passed** the shop on my bike.*
Past often begins an adverbial phrase.
*Example: I rode **past** the shop on my bike.*

Complete the sentences. Choose from past and passed.

It is six minutes ______________ midnight.

On our way to the city, we ______________ a large dairy farm.

As the balmy autumn days ______________, the maple leaves turned to gold.

Off to bed! It is ______________ your bedtime.

We rode ______________ a lake, ______________ a church and ______________ a football field.

Colour the pairs of words that are synonyms. Use a different colour for each pair.

halt	mask	glass	calm	task	waltz	wander	last
tumbler	job	roam	stop	quiet	final	cover	dance

TARGETING SPELLING 4 © PASCAL PRESS ISBN 9781925490220

UNIT 10

5 Add endings to complete the words in bold.

Wasp____ and **hornet**____ are stinging **insect**____.

I **ask**____ for two **glass**____ of orange juice.

Wearing **mask**____, the **dancer**____ **waltz**____ across the floor.

The train travelled **fast**____ and **fast**____ across the vast sandy plain.

We **bask**____ in the warm sunshine and **breath**____ in the **salt**____ air.

LOOK & LEARN

girl hair horse gym

6 Join the word parts to make compound words.

eye	time	mast	away
pass	piece	glass	brush
half	word	hair	head
class	glass	cast	land
master	mate	grass	works

7 Wave your magic wand! Write down three wishes you'd like to come true.

1 ____________________

2 ____________________

3 ____________________

8 Find and fix the spelling mistakes. Write them on the lines.

Jane washt the dishes and I dryed them. ________ ________

I saw cows and calfes wandring along the road. ________ ________

Ken holted suddenly as he past the pet shop. ________ ________

One of my daily taskes is woshing the dishes. ________ ________

Zeb saw a wasps nest and walked carmly away. ________ ________

WORD TRAPS

Don't confuse wander, which means to roam, ramble or stroll (verb); and wonder, which means to think about with curiosity (verb), awe, amazement or surprise (noun).

wander: *I love to* ***wander*** *along the beach collecting shells and pebbles.*

wonder: *I* ***wonder*** *if it will rain today.*

I often look at the star-filled sky in ***wonder***.

9 Unscramble these six insects. Start with the letter in bold.

pa**w**s l**f**ae tn**a** **h**ntoer hpp**g**aroessr fytt**b**erul

________ ________ ________ ________ ________ ________

Tricky Letter Teams: or, ear, ar

In some words, **or** has an **er** sound, as in *word* and *world*.
In some words, **ear** has an **er** sound, as in *early* and *learn*.
In some words, **ar** has an **or** sound, as in *warm* and *wharf*.

SEE & SAY

worm	work	early	learn	war	warble
word	worth	earth	yearn	wart	wharf
world	worst	earn	heard	warm	dwarf
				warn	

The plural of dwarf is usually dwarfs.

The plural of wharf can be either wharfs or wharves.

1 Add an ending to the word in bold to complete each sentence correctly.

hear We ________________ the warning sound of a fire engine.

warble The bushwalkers could hear birds ________________ in the trees.

dwarf Have you read *Snow White and the Seven* ________________?

early I arrived at the station ten minutes ________________ than Billy.

warm January is probably the ________________ month of the year.

LOOK & LEARN

since fence once dance

RULE The letter **c**, followed by an **e**, makes an **s** sound. *Examples: nice, lace, once*

2 Grow the words you know by reading these two lists of words.

race	since
face	mince
pace	dance
rice	glance
mice	prance
twice	chance

MEMORY TRAINING

Read the words in each list two times. How many words can you remember? Write them in your notebook. Check and write your scores here.

....

3 Write these compound words by joining the word parts.

clock, home, road, house, school → **work**

____
____
____
____
____

glass, steel, gas, earth, water → **works**

____
____
____
____
____

TARGETING SPELLING 4 © PASCAL PRESS ISBN 9781925490220

UNIT 11

4 Choose a word from the box to complete each sentence.

warmth
worthless
unheard
working
wordy

For hours, their cries for help went ____________________.

The teacher says the story I wrote is too ____________________.

He thought he had found a ruby, but it was a ____________________ rock.

I like to feel the ____________________ of the sun on my face in winter.

Make sure your bike is in good ____________________ order.

Adjectives can show how things compare with each other by adding **-er** or **-est**.
Examples: tall, taller, tallest
Some adjectives compare things in a special way.
Examples: good, better, best; bad, worse, worst

5 Write the correct word. Choose from bad, worse and worst.

Has the pain in your neck become ________________?

It was the ________________ cyclone of the season.

The heat has made all the bananas go ________________.

Clem's test results were the ________________ he'd ever received.

The storm grew ________________ as it approached the city.

6 Join the word parts to make compound words.

early	post	earth	hole
pass	robe	wart	men
fence	bird	cross	worm
ward	wide	worm	hog
world	word	work	word

7 Use the letters in this word to make new words.

e a r l y b i r d s

Score 1 point for each 3-letter word.
Score 3 points for each 4-letter word.
Score 5 points for each 5-letter word.

3-letter words ____

____

4-letter words ____

____

5-letter words ____

____

Letter Teams: er, ir, ur

Each letter team **er**, **ir** and **ur** represents the sound **er**.
Examples: her, person; bird, circus; curl, cursor

SEE & SAY

			Odd Bods
alert	circus	curb	journey
person	circle	cursor	journal
perform	circuit	furl	
certain	circulate	furnish	
service	whirr	pursue	
servant	whirl	purchase	

1 Write these words in their plural form.

person ______________ circus ______________ journal ______________ service ______________ circle ______________

2 Add an ending to the word in bold to complete each sentence correctly.

journey The scientists made several ____________________ to the South Pole.

purchase Dad will soon be ____________________ our tickets to the grand final.

pursue The frightened animal was being ____________________ by hunters.

whirr We heard the ____________________ sound of a helicopter overhead.

certain I would ____________________ like to go to the circus on Saturday.

edit The reporter gave her story to the ____________________ for checking.

Some words have the same sound pattern BUT are spelled differently.
Examples: keep, leap; wait, late; bone, shown

3 Read these lists of rhyming words. Pay attention to what the words *look* like.

bird	furl	burn
third	hurl	turn
heard	girl	earn
word	twirl	learn

MEMORY TRAINING

Read the words in each list two times. How many words can you remember? Write them in your notebook. Check and write your score here.

....

LOOK & LEARN

edit format check quit

TARGETING SPELLING 4 © PASCAL PRESS ISBN 9781925490220

UNIT 12

4 Colour the pairs of words that are synonyms. Use a different colour for each pair.

circle	certain	alert	journal	furl	quit	pursue	purchase
chase	diary	ring	buy	watchful	sure	fold	leave

5 Join the correct word parts to write these compound words.

sun	circle	____________	bird	word	____________
surf	wind	____________	cross	yard	____________
semi	board	____________	girl	cage	____________
whirl	burn	sunburn	church	friend	____________

6 Add the correct letter team to complete the words. Choose from ir and ur.

Jack came **f** _ _ **st** in the race and I came **th** _ _ **d**.

One **g** _ _ **l** has long **c** _ _ **ly** hair.

The large pink **b** _ _ **ds** landed gently and **f** _ _ **led** their wings.

He **t** _ _ **ned** the wheel of his car and went round in a **c** _ _ **cle**.

The **c** _ _ **cus** clown's balloons suddenly **b** _ _ **st**.

7 Join the syllables to say the words. Write a sentence about each one.

fur nit ure ____

per son al ____

ur gent ly ____

8 Join the syllables to say these words. Join them to their meaning. Use a dictionary to help you.

burg lar	peculiar or strange
fur tive	lasting for a very long time or forever
per ma nent	annoying, irritating, tiresome
fer tile	robber or thief
irk some	sly, secretive, sneaky
quirk y	able to produce well, fruitful

How many words can you remember?

Go back and choose any *See and Say* list. Read through it twice, focusing on how the words look and sound. Write as many words as you can remember in your notebook. Check how many you have written correctly and enter your score here.

Letter Teams: -er

When placed on the end of a word, the letter team **-er** is most often an 'unstressed' syllable. It has an **ŭ** sound **(uh)**. Think of it as a *lazy* sound that rolls off the end of the word.
*Examples: river = riv**uh**; silver = silv**uh**; rubber = rubb**uh***

SEE & SAY

anger	blister	whimper	lever	corner
gather	finger	whisper	cover	climber
enter	ginger	super	plaster	order
clever	panther	spider	poster	shiver

Name the pictures.

Add an ending to the word in bold to complete each sentence correctly.

gather Storm clouds are ____________________ in the west.

cover Kasim ____________________ his face with an animal mask.

order Thomas ____________________ a tasty pizza for lunch.

lever Pliers, scissors, claw hammers and tongs are all simple ____________________.

linger After she left, there was a ____________________ smell of roses in the air.

Write words of opposite meaning and find them in the word search.

shout ____________________

dull (person) ____________________

poorer ____________________

over ____________________

buyer ____________________

bigger ____________________

younger ____________________

s	c	u	r	w	c	r
e	r	n	e	h	l	e
l	o	d	h	i	e	l
l	o	e	c	s	v	l
e	k	r	i	p	e	a
r	e	p	r	e	r	m
o	l	d	e	r	k	s

TARGETING SPELLING 4 © PASCAL PRESS ISBN 9781925490220

UNIT 13

4 Complete the words by adding -er. *(Note any spelling rules.)*

It is **hot**____ in **sum**____ than it is in **wint**____.

I went to the beach with my **fath**____ and **moth**____.

Jim hit his **fing**____ with the **ham**____ instead of the nail!

My **sist**____ Kate is the best **run**____ in her class.

The **play**____**s** went on to the field for a game of **soc**____.

My country is much **cool**____ and **wet**____ than yours.

LOOK & LEARN

interesting idea extra great

5 Complete this table of adjectives and adverbs.

Adjectives (add -y)		Adverbs (add -ly)	
shiver	____________	clever	____________
butter	____________	ginger	____________
shower	____________	order	____________
slipper	____________	brother	____________
pepper	____________	tender	____________

-er is often added to **verbs** to show what some people do.
Examples: someone who *teaches* is a *teacher*; someone who *farms* is a *farmer*

6 Name the following people.

One who dances ____________

One who drives ____________

One who runs ____________

One who surfs ____________

One who writes ____________

One who plays ____________

One who buys ____________

One who gardens ____________

One who dives ____________

One who swims ____________

One who rides ____________

One who sings ____________

One who paints ____________

One who robs ____________

One who sells ____________

One who wins ____________

Sometimes, **-or** is added, not **-er**. *Examples: sailor, doctor, actor, author, editor, conductor, visitor, inventor, inspector*

7 Unscramble these 'beach' words. Begin with the letter in bold.

nasd	ahee**s**lsl	**c**arsb	vse**w**a	gl**s**aleu
______	______	______	______	______

Letter Teams: ea

The letter team **ea** has two sounds: the *long* **ea** sound, as in ***sea*** and ***team***; and the *short* **ea** sound, as in ***bread*** and ***breath***.

SEE & SAY

bread	death	feather	sweat
breadth	breath	weather	threat
spread	ready	leather	measure
thread	steady	healthy	pleasure
ahead	heavy	wealthy	treasure

1 Add endings to the words in bold to complete the sentences correctly.

measure Dad is ____________________ my room to buy new carpet.

leather The skin of a crocodile is thick and ____________________.

heavy It rained ____________________ all afternoon.

thread Mum ____________________ a needle with white cotton.

feather Parrots are well-known for their colourful ____________________.

2 Circle the correct word in the brackets.

Kasim took a deep [breadth breath] and dived overboard.

My dog is old and a bit [death deaf], so he didn't [hear here] me call him.

I don't know [whether weather] I'll pass my maths test this [weak week].

My workout at the gym has made me [sweet sweat].

I held my [breath breathe] and counted to [for four].

3 Add -ea to complete each compound word. Match it to its meaning.

h___dache	worn out, shabby (adjective)
st___dfast	all the people of a country (noun)
h___dstrong	a pain in the head (noun)
br___thtaking	one who earns money to care for their family (noun)
commonw___lth	determined to have your own way (adjective)
sw___tshirt	fixed; unchanging; faithful (adjective)
br___dwinner	causing great excitement; thrilling (adjective)
thr___dbare	a loose, light jumper (noun)

LOOK & LEARN

sugar shoe else rather

TARGETING SPELLING 4 © PASCAL PRESS ISBN 9781925490220

4 Use these letters to make a maximum of 15 words. Each word should contain **-ea** (short or long sound). The letters can only be used once in a word.

ea	r	d	f
h	t	b	s
l	w	th	er

5 Write the compound words by joining the word parts.

head – stone ______, lights ______, band ______, phones ______, first ______

head – line ______, wind ______, land ______, quarters ______, long ______

6 Choose a compound word from the lists above to complete each sentence.

Brett put on his ____________ to listen to his favourite music.

The ship sailed around the ____________ into a sheltered bay.

Here is today's ____________: *Passengers Pulled from Sinking Vessel.*

Mr Fraser went to the police ____________ to report a stolen car.

After dark, drivers switch on their car's ____________.

7 Find and fix the spelling errors. Write them on the lines.

Dad says there is stormy wether ahed. ______ ______

Jake was swetting and breafless after his race. ______ ______

The eagle spred its wings and flew steadly north. ______ ______

Mum mesurd out a tablespoon of suger. ______ ______

Tell me its length, bredth and how hevvy it is. ______ ______

8 Write about something you own that is very special to you – your personal treasure.

____

____

____

____

____

'Soft' g, ge, dge

When g is followed by an e, i or y, the letter g has a 'soft' sound (j).
*Examples: **gentle**, **giant**, **gym***

SEE & SAY

gel	stage	edge	trudge
gem	hinge	ledge	badge
gentle	fringe	hedge	bridge
cage	range	judge	ridge
page	strange	budge	dodge

1 Write these nouns in plural form.

hedge ______ page ______ bridge ______ ledge ______ gem ______

2 Add an ending to the word in bold to complete each sentence correctly.

strange It was dark and ______ quiet as we entered the forest.

judge Mrs Primm will be ______ the cake entries at the show.

gentle The boats rocked ______ on the calm waters of the lake.

dodge Gus ______ quickly when he saw a ball coming towards him.

edge Sam is ______ his way through the crowd to get a better view.

3 Join the word parts to make compound words.

stage	bridge	high	men
high	hog	stage	row
foot	coach	gentle	light
hedge	cage	hedge	stone
bird	light	gem	way

4 Name the pictures.

LOOK & LEARN

low high small which

TARGETING SPELLING 4 © PASCAL PRESS ISBN 9781925490220

5 Read these rhyming words three times each.

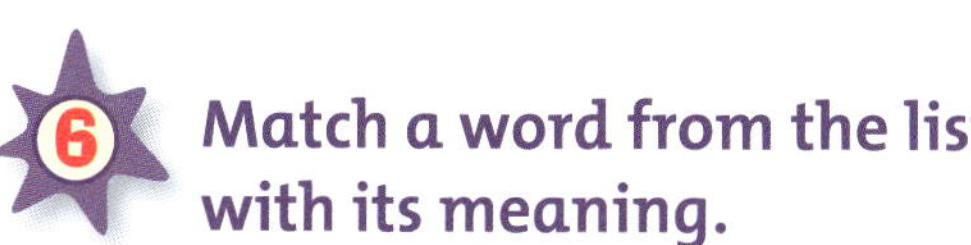

hinge singe tinge fringe cringe whinge

cage page wage rage sage stage

MEMORY TRAINING

How many words can you remember? Write them in your notebook. Check and write your scores here.

....

6 Match a word from the list above with its meaning.

_______________ money for work

_______________ to complain

_______________ anger

_______________ to burn slightly

_______________ sheet of paper in a book

_______________ a very small amount of colour

7 Colour the pairs of words that are synonyms. Use a different colour for each pair.

dodge	strange	ledge	gentle	edge	gem
kind	border	avoid	jewel	odd	shelf

8 Use the sentence clues to write the missing words, one letter in each box.

Ken jumped off the ___ of the diving board.

We crossed a ___ over the Brisbane River.

The mountain ___ was long and steep.

Her shawl had a wide ___ around the bottom.

The old gate has a broken, rusty ___.

e			
b					
r				
f					
h				

9 Use the letters in this word to make new words.

tambourines

Score 1 point for each 3-letter word.
Score 3 points for each 4-letter word.
Score 5 points for each 5-letter word.

3-letter words ______________________________

4-letter words ______________________________

5-letter words ______________________________

Letter Teams: ie, ei

The letter team **ie** has a long **e** sound. *Examples: chief, believe, piece*
The letters are turned around if they follow the letter **c**.
Examples: ceiling, receive

SEE & SAY

				Exceptions
chief	believe	niece	ceiling	their
thief	achieve	piece	deceive	weird
grief	shield	pierce	deceit	seize
relief	field	fierce	receive	vein
			receipt*	

* The **p** in *receipt* is silent. Say: 're-seat.'

1 Add an ending to the word in bold to complete each sentence correctly.

receive Diana is ________________ help from her teacher.

pierce A sharp rock ________________ the thin sides of the rubber boat.

believe There is an old saying: Seeing is ________________.

seize Jensen ________________ the rope in two hands and pulled hard.

fierce The mouse struggled ________________ to free itself from the cat's claws.

When a noun ends in **f**, follow these simple rules to write its plural.

1 If you hear an **f** sound in the plural, just add **-s**. *Examples: roof, roofs; reef, reefs*

2 If you hear a **v** sound in the plural, change **f** to **v** and add **-es**.
Examples: loaf, loaves; knife, knives; wolf, wolves

2 Write these nouns in their plural form.

field ________________ chief ________________ niece ________________

shield ________________ receipt ________________ thief ________________

3 Separate these words into nouns and verbs.

believe grieve relief deceit receipt achieve belief receive grief thieve

Nouns	Verbs
________________	________________
________________	________________
________________	________________
________________	________________
________________	________________

ie can also have a long **i** sound.
pie lie
tie die

TARGETING SPELLING 4 © PASCAL PRESS ISBN 9781925490220

UNIT 16

4 Colour the pairs of words that are synonyms. Use a different colour for each pair.

fierce	seize	weird	thief	piece	achieve	grief
bit	reach	savage	sorrow	grab	strange	robber

LOOK & LEARN

fall hall wall by buy

Generally, write **i** before **e** *except* after **c**. *Examples: piece, field, chief* **BUT** *ceiling, receive, conceit*. More exceptions: *their, weird, seize, vein, foreign*

5 Fill in the missing letters. Choose from ie and ei.

I **bel** _ _ **ve** you sent me a parcel, but I didn't **rec** _ _ **ve** it.

The **sh** _ _ **ld** will be won or lost on the football **f** _ _ **ld**.

Jenny **rec** _ _ **ved** a top prize for her **p** _ _ **ce** of poetry.

The **th** _ _ **f** could not get past the **f** _ _ **rce** guard dog.

The **ch** _ _ **f** editor checked the **br** _ _ **f** news article.

6 Join the word parts to make compound words.

field	field	wall	piece
water	piece	field	way
battle	case	corn	work
time	mouse	master	field
brief	fall	hall	paper

7 Write sentences to show how the words shield and field can be used 1. as a noun and 2. as a verb.

1 ____

2 ____

1 ____

2 ____

How many words can you remember?

Go back and choose any *See and Say* list. Read through it twice, focusing on how the words look and sound. Write as many words as you can remember in your notebook. Check how many you have written correctly and enter your score here.

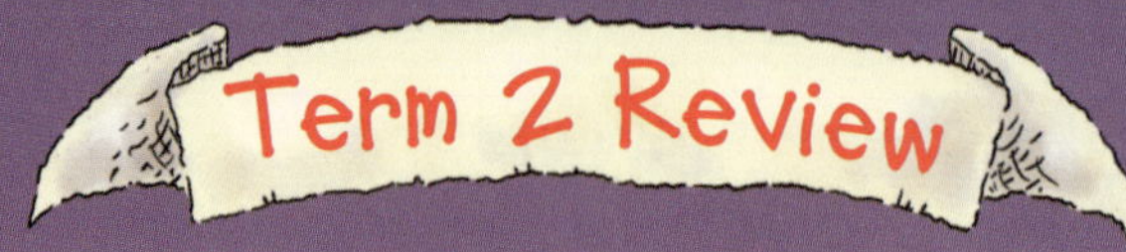

1 Name the pictures.

2 Write these nouns in plural form.

world	____________	half	____________	circus	____________
hedge	____________	chief	____________	claw	____________
page	____________	field	____________	breath	____________
idea	____________	circle	____________	waltz	____________

3 Write antonyms *(words of opposite meaning)* for these words.

first	____________	slow	____________	boy	____________
exit	____________	sell	____________	shout	____________
low	____________	best	____________	dark	____________
large	____________	cool	____________	poor	____________

4 Complete this table.

	Add -ing	Add -ed	Add -er
learn	learning	learned	learner
perform			
wander			
range			
warble			
pursue			
achieve			
fence			

TARGETING SPELLING 4 © PASCAL PRESS ISBN 9781925490220

Unit 1

1 king, crab, ants, branch, tent, frog, stamp, shell, brush, ring

2 smelling, grabbing, locking, blinking, stepping, dragged, cracked, skipped, stretched, dropped

3 thicker, stronger; bunches, crusty; splashed, strongly; running, skipping; frosty, thickest (thicker)

4 Memory Training: him, rim, dim, grim, swim, brim, trim; pump, lump, clump, dump, hump, stump, slump; lock, mock, dock, shock, stock, flock, block

5 trinket: a small ornament such as a piece of jewellery; scatter: to throw all over the place; ringlet: a long curly strand of hair; scamper: to run or hurry away quickly; blanket: a large piece of cloth used as a bed covering

6 swam, sent, fell, went, sang, ran, rang, got, sat, had

7 Writing activity

Unit 2

1 place, plane, plate, made, make, male, mane, mate, tile, time, tide, tine, tire, same, sane, sale, safe, sage, sake, sate, save, rode, role, robe, rose, rope, rove

2 scraping, scraped; shining, shone; making, made; amusing, amused; trading, traded; hoping, hoped; riding, rode; exploding, exploded; shaking, shook; racing, raced; sliding, slid

3 Memory Training: make, cake, lake, fake, flake, rake, shake, snake, quake, brake; nice, rice, mice, dice, lice, slice, spice, twice, price, advice

4 spicy, stony, lacy, shady, shiny, rosy, tasty, slimy, smoky, racy; nicely, gamely, gravely, closely, lately, safely, wisely, finely, timely, bravely

5 Writing activity

6 rosebuds, fireplace, grapevine, facebook, spaceship, snakeskin, cheesecake, earthquake, milkshake, takeaway

7 explosion: a loud outburst; confusion: state of being muddled or mixed up; erosion: the slow wearing away by wind or water; global: relating to the whole world; final: coming at the end; last.

Unit 3

1 displayed, planes, container, weighs, grams, making, wading, trains, buses, delayed, flooding (floods), grating, chopping, finely

2 Do, does; did, done; does, do; Did, done; do, does

3 pale, tail, plane, sale, reign, eight, made, main, weigh, bale

4 Memory Training: ate, mate, late, date, gate, hate, rate, grate, skate; rain, main, pain, train, grain, brain, slain, stain, strain

5 one, two, three, four, five, six, seven, eight, nine, ten

6 decay-rot; rule-reign; contain-hold; lift-raise; stay-remain; show-display; explain-tell

7 grate, dice, skate, frozen, wade, waves, tide, make, plane, place, game

8 daylight, daytime, daybreak, daydream, daybed; playground, playpen, plaything, playroom, playtime

Unit 4

1 squeezing, greasy, clearly, reaping, freezer

2 seashell, seashore, seaweed, seaside, seafood, seabed

3 beehive, teardrops, peanuts, seatbelt, mealtime, teapot, seedpod, weekend, treehouse, steamboat, wheelchair, beekeeper

4 near, early, hard, push, asleep, sweet, full

5 peel, meal, week, cheap, reel, creek, cheer, team, been, seals, heel, heal

6 cease-stop; reason-excuse; peer-look; animal-creature; near-close; easy-simple; steer-guide

7 referee: person who makes sure players follow the rules of a game; weasel: a small animal that eats mice and rabbits; beacon: a signal showing the way or warning of danger; beachcomber: person who gathers things washed up by the sea; peevish: cross, easily annoyed

8 Writing activity

Unit 5

1 noses, crows, loads, coasts, bones, meadows, loaves, elbows, shadows

2 snowflakes, flagpole, toadstool, rosebud, scarecrow

3 rode, grew, drove, blew, shook, wrote, knew, made, stole, rose

4 follows, shadow, raincoat, soaking, arrows, bow, coach, tomorrow, shoal, approaching, coast

5 find, poor, close (shut), narrow, slow

6 rosy, snowy, closely, stony, slowly, lonely

7 Memory Training: mow, row, bow, know, show, blow, flow, grow, crow; bone, lone, cone, tone, phone, hone, stone, drone, throne

8 Examples: 3-letter: ail, ale, ant, ate, can, cat, cot, eat, ice, let, lit, lot, net, nit, not, oat, oil, one, sat, sea, set, sit, tan, tea, ten, til, tin, toe

4-letter: anti, ants, cane, case, cast, cent, coal, coat, coin, colt, cone, cost, east, into, lace, lane,

TARGETING SPELLING 4 © PASCAL PRESS ISBN 9781925490220

last, late, lean, lent, lice, line, lint, list, loan, lone, lost, nail, neat, nest, nice, nits, nose, note, oats, oils, sail, sale, salt, sane, scat, seal, seat, sent, silt, slat, slit, slot, soil, tail, tale, tile, toes, toil

5-letter: aisle, clean, cleat, clone, coast, inlet, inset, leant, least, saint, salon, scale, scent, scone, slain, slant, stain, stale, steal, stile, stole, stone, tails, tales, talon, tiles, tines, toils, tonal, tones, tonic

Unit 6

1 fights, flies, cries, lives, knives, kites, pies, ties, lies

2 hiking, kindest, slightly, shiny, mightier

3 sunlight, daylight, moonlight, bedlight, lamplight, spotlight, headlight, candlelight, flashlight, footlight

4 wild, light (fair), white, dry, wide (broad), night, find, right, bright, kind (nice)

5 where (when), when; what, where; who, what; why, where; what, who

6 dries, drying, dried; fries, frying, fried; tries, trying, tried; spies, spying, spied
lies, lying, lied (lay); dies, dying, died

7 flying, shine, knife, five, blind, hive, nine, riding

Unit 7

1 feet, geese, hoofs (hooves), groups, teeth, roofs

2 flew, shook, knew, lost, threw, blew, grew, chose, took, drew

3 toothache, moonlight, schoolground, screwdriver, bookmark, goodbye

4 Memory Training: new, dew, few, flew, blew, brew, crew, grew, drew, screw, threw, chew, knew, stew, strew, spew

5 can't, don't, isn't, won't, aren't

6 footpath, football, footbridge, footloose, footstoool, footsteps, footprints, footlights

7 door, tooth, foot, roof, hook, flood

8 don't, soup; someone, wooden; knew, jewels; isn't, group; can't, flooded

9 possum, koala, kangaroo, platypus, echidna

Unit 8

1 hours, down, foul, flour, bowl, now, flower, Write, piece

2 Memory Training: town, gown, brown, crown, clown, drown, frown; out, pout, spout, scout, stout, snout, shout; round, found, sound, hound, bound, wound, ground

3 downstairs, downtown, downstream, downwind, downlight, downhill; outdoors, outside, outbreak, outburst, outline, outskirts

4 surrounded, pronounce, soundlessly, announce, mountainous

5 crowd, fountain, town, found, cowering, growling, cloudy, showers, hours, bounded, pouch, mountains, shouted, loudly

6 down, poor, found, good, sour, closed, south, bright, loud

7 coward: person eager to avoid danger, pain or difficulty; boundary: the border, edge or limit of something; astounded: amazed, astonished, stunned; southward: moving towards the south; announcement: information told or made known to the public

Term 1 review

1 flag, fire, door, moon, lightning, peach, train, whale, rake, sheep

2 bunches, mice, lives, feet, cracks, loaves, groups, deer, tides, cries, leaves, teeth

3 near (close), safe, leave, clean, thin (slim, skinny), early, full, pull, easy (soft), sweet, slow, dry

4 rode, wrote, froze, grew, took, slid, flew, chose, knew, shone, shook, bit

5 paintbrush, wheelbarrow, peanuts, coastline, beehive, moonlight, football, grapevine, bookshelf, rainbow, underground, weekend, mousetrap, roundabout, snowflakes, soundwaves

6 road, creek; whale, great, sea; made, right, main; four, plain, tied; Two, ate, whole

7 dragging, skating, dying, stepping; dried, chewed, dropped, refused; winner, stretcher, rubber, swimmer

8 smelly, grubby, spicy, rosy, greasy, shiny, shaky, skinny, nosy, funny, sandy, racy

9 peered, sea, creatures, clear; season, leaves; squeezed, sweet, cheese; hear, cheering, teams; seashells, seaweed, beach

10 reindeer, sleigh, early, around, cried, lost, Where, tomorrow, hasn't, done

Unit 9

1 lawnmower, jawbone, sawmill, scoreboard, drawbridge, bushwalk, cornflakes, shoreline

2 Memory Training: saw, jaw, paw, law, raw, claw; born, corn, horn, torn, worn, shorn

3 causing, soared, drawers, scoring, coarsely, beginning

4 1 scornful: showing disgust or contempt; 2 tawdry: cheap, showy, gaudy; 3 storage: a place to keep things; 4 dormant: not active as if asleep or resting; 5 boredom: state of being tired or weary of something

5 Correct answers: roar, soar, stork, caught, Pour, horse, roar, court, horse, course

6 taught, drew, wore, knew, saw, tore, flew, shook, shot, blew, shone, caught
7 Writing/discussion activity
8 Writing activity

Unit 10

1 calves, glasses, waltzes, wasps, halves, classes
2 ask, task, mask, bask, flask; past, fast, cast, mast, blast; pass, class, glass, grass, brass
3 past, passed, passed, past, past, past, past
4 halt-stop, mask-cover, glass-tumbler, calm-quiet, task-job, waltz-dance, wander-roam, last-final
5 Wasps, hornets, insects; asked, glasses; masks, dancers, waltzed; faster, faster; basked, breathed, salty
6 password, halftime, classmate, masterpiece, masthead, glassworks, hairbrush, castaway, grassland
7 Writing activity
8 washed, dried, calves, wandering, halted, passed, tasks, washing, wasp's (wasps'), calmly
9 wasp, flea, ant, hornet, grasshopper, butterfly

Unit 11

1 heard, warbling, Dwarfs, earlier, warmest
2 Memory Training
3 clockwork, homework, roadwork, housework, schoolwork; glassworks, steelworks, gasworks, earthworks, waterworks
4 unheard, wordy, worthless, warmth, working
5 worse, worst, bad, worst, worse
6 password, fencepost, wardrobe, worldwide, earthworm, warthog, crossword, wormhole, workmen
7 Examples: 3-letter: aid, ail, air, ale, are, bad, bar, bay, bed, bid, bye, dab, day, dry, lad, lay, led, lid, lie, ray, red, rib, rid, sad, say, sea, sir, sly, yes

4-letter: bade, bail, bale, bare, bear, bird, bled, bray, bred, dais, dare, days, dear, dial, dire, dray, earl, ears, laid, lair, lard, lead, lied, raid, rail, read, real, rile, rise, said, seal, sire

5-letter: aired, baled, bared, based, beady, beard, blade, braid, bread, bride, daily, dairy, dares, deals, delay, diary, dries, early, laird, layer, rabid, raids, rails, raise, reads, relay, riled, sabre, sadly, sidle, sired, slide, years, yield

Unit 12

1 persons (people), circuses, journals, services, circles
2 journeys, purchasing, pursued, whirring, certainly, editor
3 Memory Training
4 circle-ring; certain-sure; alert-watchful; journal-diary; furl-fold; quit-leave; pursue-chase; purchase-buy
5 surfboard, semicircle, whirlwind, birdcage, crossword, girlfriend, churchyard
6 first, third, girl, curly, birds, furled, turned, circle, circus, burst
7 Writing activity
8 furtive: sly, secretive, sneaky; permanent: lasting for a very long time or forever; fertile: able to produce well, fruitful; irksome: annoying, irritating, tiresome; quirky: peculiar or strange

Unit 13

1 spider, finger, climber, shiver, panther
2 gathering, covered, ordered, levers, lingering
3 whisper, clever, richer, under, seller, smaller, older
4 hotter, summer, winter; father, mother; finger, hammer; sister, runner; players, soccer; cooler, wetter
5 shivery, buttery, showery, slippery, peppery; cleverly, gingerly, orderly, brotherly, tenderly
6 dancer, driver, runner, surfer, writer, player, buyer, gardener, diver, swimmer, rider, singer, painter, robber, seller, winner
7 sand, seashell, crabs, waves, seagull

Unit 14

1 measuring, leathery, heavily, threaded, feathers
2 breath, deaf, hear, whether, week, sweat, breath, four
3 steadfast: fixed, unchanging, faithful; headstrong: determined to have your own way; breathtaking: causing great excitement, thrilling; commonwealth: all the people of a country; sweatshirt: a loose, light jumper; breadwinner: one who earns money to care for their family; threadbare: worn out, shabby
4 Possible words (short sound): read, deaf, head, weather, breast, bread, feather, lead, threat, thread, wear, bear, leather; (long sound): read, fear, seat, tear, lead, heat, seal, deal, beat, beast, leaf, wheat, east
5 headstone, headlights, headband, headphones, headfirst, headline, headwind, headland, headquarters, headlong
6 headphones, headland, headline, headquarters, headlights
7 weather, ahead, sweating, breathless, spread, steadily, measured, sugar, breadth, heavy
8 Writing activity

Unit 15

1 hedges, pages, bridges, ledges, gems
2 strangely, judging, gently, dodged, edging
3 highlight, footbridge, hedgehog, birdcage, highway, stagelight, gentlemen, hedgerow, gemstone
4 bridge, cage, judge, badge, stage
5 Memory Training
6 wage, whinge, rage, singe, page, tinge
7 dodge-avoid; strange-odd; ledge-shelf; gentle-kind; edge-border; gem-jewel
8 edge, bridge, ridge (range), fringe, hinge
9 Examples:
3-letter: aim, ant, are, arm, art, ate, ban, bar, bat, bet, bin, bit, bun, bus, ear, eat, man, mar, mat, men, met, mob, nab, net, nib, nit, nor, not, nut, oat, orb, our, out, ram, ran, rat, rib, rim, rob, rot, rub, run, sat, sea, set, sin, sir, sit, sob, son, sun, tab, tan, tar, tea, tin, tis, ton, tub
4-letter: ants, arts, bait, bare, barn, base, beam, bear, beat, bent, best, boat, bone, bore, born, bout, bran, brat, brim, ears, east, eats, into, iron, item, main, mare, mast, mate, mean, meat, mine, mint, mire, mist, moan, moat, more, most, name, near, neat, nest, nose, numb, ours, oust, rain, rant, rate, ream, rest, rise, roam, roan, robe, robs, rose, same, sane, sent, sire, snob, soar, sobs, some, sort, sour, stab, star, stem, sure, tame, team, tear, time, tire, tone, tour, tram, trim, tube
5-letter: about, amber, beast, boast, brain, bream, brine, burnt, burst, earns, inset, inter, irons, manor, mason, means, meant, miner, minor, miser, mourn, names, orbit, raise, reins, rinse, risen, roast, robes, rouse, route, routs, ruins, sabre, siren, smart, snare, snore, snout, stain, stare, stone, store, timer, times, tines, train, tries, tubes, umber, unmet

Unit 16

1 receiving, pierced, believing, seized, fiercely
2 fields, shields, chiefs, receipts, nieces, thieves
3 Nouns: relief, deceit, receipt, belief, grief. Verbs: believe, grieve, achieve, receive, thieve
4 fierce-savage; seize-grab; weird-strange; piece-bit; achieve-reach; grief-sorrow
5 believe, receive, shield, field, received, piece, thief, fierce, chief, brief
6 waterfall, battlefield, timepiece, briefcase, wallpaper, fieldwork, cornfield, masterpiece, hallway
7 Writing activity

Term 2 review

1 masks, worm, fence, spider, bread, bridge, bird, palm, feather, cage
2 worlds, hedges, pages, ideas, halves, chiefs, fields, circles, circuses, claws, breaths, waltzes
3 last, enter, high, small, fast, buy, worst, warm, girl, whisper, light (fair), rich (wealthy)
4 performing, performed, performer; wandering, wandered, wanderer; ranging, ranged, ranger; warbling, warbled, warbler; pursuing, pursued, pursuer; achieving, achieved, achiever; fencing, fenced, fencer
5 sunglasses, hedgehog, gingerbread (man), lawnmower, headphones
6 halt, breadth, strange, applaud, certain, fierce, high, thief, pursue, wealthy, board, last
7 calf, shoes (boots), climber, feathers, half, wallet, bridge, thief (robber), field, corner
8 leather, red, heavy, measure, length, breadth, breath, headfirst, fed, bread, wet, weather, ahead, west

Unit 17

1 saddle, rocket, candle, chicken, bottle
2 twinkling, trembled, nibbling, sizzling, rumbled, huddling (huddled)
3 wickets, pocket, puddles, tickets, jungle
4 Memory Training: rumble, mumble, tumble, bumble, fumble, humble, grumble, crumble, stumble
5 settler: a person who chooses to live in a new area or country; muffler: a warm scarf; tumbler: 1 a drinking glass, 2 a gymnast; angler: a person who fishes with a hook and line; wriggler: common name for a mosquito larva; bubbler: a drinking fountain
6 saddlebag, bluebottle, pocketknife, bumblebee, paddleboat, candlestick
7 Writing activity
8 shuffle, bottle, sample, juggles, puddle, ruffled, settled, bundle, wrinkled

Unit 18

1 moments, beginning, finally, stabled, saddles, bridles, Soldiers, rifles, stationed, rooftops, studded, rubies
2 finally, ably, recently, vocally, totally, vibrantly, secretly, stupidly, silently
3 Writing activity
4 giant: huge, enormous; vibrate: move back and forth quickly, shake, tremble; major: greater in importance; photo: a picture taken with a camera; locust: an insect like a grasshopper
5 Correct words: bridal, staple, title, Solar, radar
6 baker, apron, clothing, favourite, event, metre, music, later, July, Pluto, tiny, frozen, kilometres, soloist, microphone
7 tulip-flower; student-pupil; human-person; pirate-robber; baby-infant; donate-give; lady-woman
8 Examples: 3-letter words: air, ant, ape, are, art,

TARGETING SPELLING 4 © PASCAL PRESS ISBN 9781925490220

ate, can, cap, car, cat, cop, cot, ear, eat, ice, its, nap, net, nip, not, oar, oat, opt, pan, par, pat, pea, pen, pet, pin, pit, pot, ran, rap, rat, rip, rot, sac, sap, sat, sea, set, sin, sip, sir, sit, son, sop, tan, tap, tar, tea, ten, tin, tip, tis, toe, ton, top

4-letter words: acre, airs, ants, apes, arts, cane, cape, carp, cart, case, cast, cent, coat, cone, cope, core, corn, ears, east, eats, into, nape, near, neat, nest, nice, nose, note, pain, pair, pane, pant, pass, past, peas, pert, pine, pint, poet, pore, port, post, race, rain, rant, rate, reap, rent, rest, rice, ripe, rips, roan, rope, rots, sane, scat, sent, soap, sort, star, stop, tape, taps, tart, tear, tent, test, tint, tips, tire, toes, tone, toss, trap, trip

5-letter words: acorn, acres, aeons, apron, arise, arose, asset, aster, attic, canes, cares, carts, casts, cater, coast, coats, coins, cones, cores, crane, crate, cress, crest, crone, cross, inset, inter, irate, irons, nears, noses, notes, opens, orate, orcas, paces, pacts, pains, paint, pairs, panic, parse, parts, paste, pears, pines, pints, poets, pores, posts, price, pries, print, prise, races, rains, rates, reaps, reins, rents, rests, rises, ropes, scans, scant, scent, scone, score, scrap, sites, spare, spate, spice, spine, spins, spite, spore, sport, stain, start, stone, store, strip, tapes, tarts, taste, tears, tents, trace, train, traps, treat

Unit 19

1 families, monkeys, cities, valleys, countries, libraries, donkeys, cherries, duties, chimneys, stories, gullies

2 sturdier, dizzier, bumpier, cloudier, steadier; dirtiest, cosiest, cuddliest, funniest, happiest; busily, daintily, crazily, prettily, ordinarily

3 obeys, obeying, obeyed; replies, replying, replied; annoys, annoying, annoyed; studies, studying, studied; carries, carrying, carried; buries, burying, buried

4 saw, seen, done, has, went, gone, see, went, did, went

5 rely-depend; duty-task; country-nation; reply-answer; story-tale; annoy-irritate; frisky-playful

6 Grammar activity

7 Writing activity

Unit 20

1 knot, knock(ing), knob, kneel(ing), knight

2 writing, knives, wrongly, knitting, knotted, knobbly

3 wristwatch, kneecap, shipwreck, doorknob, knockout, knitwear, pocketknife, knighthood, kneepads, doorknocker, swordfish

4 answer, wrong, beautiful, dirty, whisper, first, later, best

5 know, road; kneads, bread; knew, right, way; Wring, clothes; tied, knot

6 writhe-squirm; wren-bird; wrath-anger; wreathe-surround; wrap-enclose; wrench-twist; wreck-ruin

7 1: a skite or boastful person; 2: a handle for a door or drawer; 3: finger joint near the hand; 4: a pretty ornament; 5: a rounded hill; 6: a particular skill; 7: a rascal, rogue or scoundrel; 8: learning

Unit 21

1 comb, thistle, thumb, castle, lamb

2 whistling, listens, doubtful, glistened (glistens), combed, rustling

3 wrestler, listener, writer, wringer, fastener, climber, whistler, knitter, knocker, wrapper

4 whistle, combing, nestling, debt, listened, lambs

5 dumbbell: hand-held weight; thistledown: light, feathery material; breadcrumbs: small pieces of broken bread; sandcastle: model of a castle built in sand; cockscomb: 1 crest on head of rooster 2 a red-flowering garden plant

6 false, true, false, false, true, true, true, false

7 kid, foal, lamb, puppy, calf, fawn, cub, piglet

Unit 22

1 boys, appointed, moistened, wiped, annoyed, avoiding, girls, joined, enjoying, noisy, spoiled, started

2 loyal-faithful; join-connect; destroy-ruin; avoid-dodge; royal-regal; annoy-bother; moist-damp

3 spoil, hoist, avoid, choice, joyful, poison, coin, boil: MOSQUITO

4 android: a robot that looks and moves like a human; decoy: something used to lure someone into danger or into a trap; turquoise: 1 blue-green colour 2 mineral prized as a gemstone; asteroid: one of thousands of small, solid bodies that orbit the sun; turmoil: extreme confusion, disorder

5 Roy, joined, Royal, boy, poisonous, coiled, voices, noisy, Annoying, spoiled, employer, appointed

6 royalty, joyfully, joyously, pointer, destroyer, loyalty, appointment, avoidable, avoidance, employment

7 Examples: 3-letter: aft, ail, ale, ate, eat, fat, fit, let, lit, sat, sea, set, sit, tea, tie, vat, vet

4-letter: ails, east, eats, evil, fail, fast, feat, file, fist, five, lass, last, left, less, life, lift, list, live, safe, sail, sale, salt, save, seal, seat, sift, silt, slat, slit, tail, tale, teal, ties, tile, vale, vast, veal, veil, vest, vile

5-letter: aisle, alive, evils, fails, feast, files, fists, fives, least, lifts, lives, sails, sales, salve, seals, seats, sifts, slate, slats, slave, slits, stale, stave, steal, stile, svelt, tails, tales, tiles, vales, valet, veils, vials, vista, vital

Unit 23

1 squares, fairies, pairs, parents, dairies
2 preparing, compared, dairying (dairies), barely, fairly, daring
3 hairy, hairless, fairly, fairness, careless, careful
4 Writing activity
5 barefoot, warehouse, hardware, staircase, software, caretaker, downstairs, stairway, scarecrow
6 quiet, dairy, bare, hair, flare, night, fairy, flower, hair, fare, stairs, team, fair
7 wears, wearing, wore, compares, comparing, compared; tears, tearing, tore; prepares, preparing, prepared; stares, staring, stared; swears, swearing, swore
8 Writing activity
9 hare, dairy, parents, mare, fare

Unit 24

1 along, away, aloud, ago, around, afraid, ahead
2 asleep, aboard, ashore, ablaze, away, aglow, avoid, afloat, afar, aloft, alone, ashamed, apart, aware
3 along, alive, around, above, about, again
4 already, all ready; all right; all together; all ready, already; altogether; alright, all together
5 Memory Training: awash, amid, arise, abound, await, anew, adrift, afresh
6 ajar: partly open; akimbo: standing with hands on hips, elbows out; abreast: side by side; astride: with the legs on either side of something; avert: to turn away from

Term 3 review

1 pear, sword, bucket, square, castle, bridge, bear, comb, table, chicken
2 lambs, knives, fairies, cities, ankles, rubies, voices, stories, families, thistles, monkeys, crumbs
3 false, gentle (smooth), ahead, most, answer, wrong (left), alive, front, dirty, evening (afternoon), country, beginning (start)
4 weather, clothes, write, tale, knight, hair, pair, bridle, horse, know, mayor
5 scarecrow, dumbbell, sandcastle, gingerbread (man), hairbrush
6 relies, relying, relied; knits, knitting, knitted; prepares, preparing, prepared; writes, writing, wrote; wears, wearing, wore; catches, catching, caught
7 bucket, evening, always, final, begin, story, hurry, beautiful, rely, answer, listen, scared
8 gentleness (gently, gentler), amazement, wrestler, enjoyment (enjoyable), beautiful, busyness (business, busily), avoidable, scarcely, bearable, employer (employment, employable), amusement, climber (climbable)
9 chicken, dairy, animals, two, square, money, kitchen, bridle, knob, station

Unit 25

1 guests, queries, guitars, guides, guesses
2 guessed, disguised, moved, quickly, quietly, Queues, gathered, penguins, being, squealed, strumming, guitars, Mosquitoes, quickly, ponds, puddles
3 quit-leave; guide-steer; query-question; guest-visitor; guard-protect; quiet-silent; quest-search
4 queuing, queued, guessing, guessed, disguising, disguised, querying, queried, guiding, guided, squealing, squealed, quitting, quit
5 quartet: group of four people; quaff: drink down thirstily; quiver: tremble or shake; case for holding arrows; quench: satisfy, extinguish; quill: large feather; old-fashioned feather pen; spine of echidna; squad: group taking part in a shared activity; squander: to spend or use wastefully
6 Writing activity
7 mouthguard, guidebook, earthquake, lifeguard, guesswork, quicksand, quarterfinal
8 quiet, quite; quite, quite; quite, quiet; quiet, quite; quiet, quite

Unit 26

1 camels, medals, models, labels, angels
2 labelled, snorkelling, tunnels, modelling, finally
3 locally, visually, usually, annually, totally, normally, physically, manually, mentally, orally, legally, magically
4 towel, squirrel, funnel, barrel, kennel
5 vocal: having to do with the voice; fatal: causing death; deadly; penal: of or involving punishment; spinal: concerning the spine or backbone; vital: necessary for life; essential; very important; frugal: careful not to waste anything; thrifty
6 anywhere, anyhow, anything, anybody; somewhere, somehow, something, somebody; everywhere, everyone, everything, everybody
7 travel, hotels, motels, historical, novel, physical, pummel, medal, final, carnival, corals, petals
8 Writing activity

Unit 27

1 ploughs (ploughed), planting, coughing, does, really, animals, roughly, thoughtful, manners, lately, lives
2 bough-branch; drought-famine; bought-purchased; trough-trench; tough-strong; enough-plenty; rough-bumpy
3 Writing activity
4 fought, bought, sought, thought, brought, taught, caught, drew, swam, kept

TARGETING SPELLING 4 © PASCAL PRESS ISBN 9781925490220

5 already, fought, won, bear, bough, plane, through, deer, doe, mare, pair, bought, quite

6 enough, drought, brought, trough, thought, until, though, sought, through: THESAURUS

7 Examples: 3-letter: age, ago, are, art, ash, ate, ear, eat, far, fat, foe, fog, for, gas, get, goo, got, hag, has, hat, her, hot, hug, hut, oar, oat, off, ore, out, rag, rat, rot, rug, sat, set, tar, the, toe, too, tug, use, ute

4-letter: ears, east, fare, fast, fate, fear, foot, fore, fort, four, fret, gash, gate, gear, goes, gush, hare, hate, hear, heat, host, hour, huge, oats, ogre, oust, raft, rage, rate, rear, roof, root, rose, safe, shut, sofa, soot, sore, sort, sour, sure, tear, thug, thus, toes, tore, tour, true, user

5-letter: after, argue, aster, fares, fears, feast, forth, forts, fours, fresh, frets, frost, gates, gears, ghost, goose, grate, great, guest, gusto, hares, haste, hears, heart, hoots, horse, hours, house, ogres, other, ought, outer, roost, roots, rouge, rough, rouse, route, shaft, share, shear, shoot, short, shout, shrug, south, stage, stare, store, sugar, those, tough, trash

Unit 28

1 throbbing, whiskers, triumphantly, photos, whimpering, thronged

2 throbbing, throbbed; whining, whined; throwing, threw; whinging (whingeing), whinged; thinking, thought; whimpering, whimpered

3 throng-crowd; photo-image; myth-legend; whiff-puff; thrust-push; whinge-complain; thorough-complete

4 whirlwind, whitecaps, wheelchair, wheelbarrow, whalebone, whenever, whirlpool

5 orphan: a child without parents; typhoon: a tropical cyclone or hurricane; whittle: to shape a piece of wood with a sharp knife; whinny: the sound made by a horse; python: a large, long snake that wraps around its prey; enthrall: captivate or enchant

6 thump, alphabet, whisker, throw, hyphen, photo, these, thirsty, whale, through, white, phrase, them, phone, wheel, thing, whole, elephant, whisper, python

Unit 29

1 updated, downloaded, uprooted, uplifting, downplayed

2 downplay, uphold, downtime, uproot, upstanding, upon, downfall, uprising, upend, downcast, upset, downtrodden, downpour, upsurge, downslide, upcoming

3 upriver, downriver; upload, download; upside, downside; upwind, downwind, upbeat, downbeat; upsize, downsize; upswing, downswing; upstage, downstage

4 downstairs, uphill, downstream, upended, download, upgrade, downpour, downtown

5 outside, outbound, outfield, outboard, inbox, input, inflow, ingoing, inlet

6 upsurge, upset, downtime, upcoming, downpipe

7 Examples: 3-letter: and, ant, are, arm, art, awe, dam, den, dew, don, dot, ear, eat, end, era, mad, man, mar, mat, men, met, mow, net, new, nod, not, now, oar, oat, ode, ore, owe, own, ram, ran, rat, raw, red, rod, row, sat, saw, sea, set, sew, sod, sow, tan, tar, tea, ten, toe, ton, tow, wad, war, wet, woe, won

4-letter: ants, arms, arts, atom, dame, dams, dare, date, dawn, dear, does, dome, done, dots, down, draw, drew, ears, east, eats, ends, made, mane, mast, mate, mats, mean, meat, moan, moat, mode, more, morn, most, name, near, neat, nest, news, node, nose, note, oats, owes, rate, rats, read, ream, rest, road, roam, roan, rode, rose, rote, rots, sand, seam, seat, sewn, snow, some, sore, sown, star, stem, stow, swam, swan, swat, tame, team, tear, tend, toad, toes, tore, torn, town, tows, wade, wane, want, wart, wean, wear, wend, went, west, worn, wren

5-letter: amend, armed, aster, dames, dares, dates, deans, domes, dotes, dream, drown, endow, manes, mates, means, meant, meats, moans, mowed, named, names, nears, notes, omens, onset, owned, owner, rated, roads, roams, roast, rowed, sated, smart, smear, stare, steam, stern, store, storm, swear, swore, sworn, tamed, towed, towns, tread, wader, wades, wands, wanes, wants, wares, waste, water, wears, woman, women, worse, worst, wrote

Unit 30

1 underline, overboard, underwater, underweight, overseas, overgrown

2 overload, overlook, overdue, overspend, overflow, overwork; undercoat, undersize, undergrowth, underbelly, underpay, undergo

3 underrate, underpaid, underripe, underpriced, undercooked, underlay, underachieve, underpopulated

4 overtaken, overlooking, overturned, undertaking, overflowed, undergoing

5 overjoyed, overhead, overcoat, undercurrent, Overnight, overcast, overarm, Underwater

6 overwrought: extremely excited or agitated; overrule: to reject or decide against someone's ideas; overhang: to jut out over something; understorey: the plants growing beneath the canopy of a forest; undermine: to erode or dig under the earth's surface causing it to weaken; undertow: a strong current below the surface of the waves; undercover: working in secret

7 Writing activity

Unit 31

1 recovering, recovered; removing, removed; reflecting, reflected; regretting, regretted; depending, depended; deleting, deleted; descending, descended; describing, described

2 regroup, retell, report, relay, review, retail, replay, reform, reverse, reply; derail, debate, delay, defuse, declare, delight, detail, debrief, decay, deport

3 departure, replacement, removable, regrettable, recovery, removal, defendable, deletion

4 deplete: to use most of something; deter: to prevent or advise against doing; deny: to say something is not true; refuse; resume: to continue; to take up again after a pause; revert: to go back to a former habit, belief, practice or condition; devise: to invent or plan something; repel: to drive back; to keep something away

5 revise, delay; retail, reduced; report, deserved; reduce, resist; Refer, detain

6 detour, repaired; wasn't, recover; regretted, descend; types, reduced; passed, rebuilt

7 car, bike, bus, truck, boat, ferry, train, plane

Unit 32

1 illustration, nation, option, station, fraction, lotion, collection, expedition, fiction, relation

2 reaction, creation, prevention, exhaustion, deletion, reflection, population, invention, operation, celebration, location, subtraction

3 portion: a part or a share of something; edition: one printing of a book, magazine or newspaper; caption: a title or an explanation for a picture or illustration; intention: a firm plan or purpose; exception: someone or something that is different from all the others

4 exceptional, optional, intentional, national, additional, educational, fictional, functional, emotional, traditional

5 ed u ca tion; com pet i tion; in vit a tion; sta tion; ill us tra tions; pop u la tion

6 loosens, loosening, loosened; fastens, fastening, fastened; tightens, tightening, tightened, ties, tying, tied

Term 4 Review

1 guitar, elephant, graph, mosquito, penguin

2 myths, guesses, questions, boughs, models, disguises, fractions, throngs, options, queries, detours, relations

3 overarm, tight, first, unusual, downgrade, underweight, guilty, upstream, soft (quiet), empty, fiction, nephew

4 quite, bought; whether, passed; guest, brought; quiet, angel; weather, quite; though, past

5 levels, levelling, levelled; queries, querying, queried; deserves, deserving, deserved; throbs, throbbing, throbbed; regrets, regretting, regretted; guides, guiding, guided

6 whistle, tunnel, cattle, gravel, camel, unusual, animal, snorkel, coral, people, feral, animals, local, final, oval

7 overgrown, downhill, overboard, underwater, uprooted, overturned, overarm, underarm

8 dependable, fictional, removable, optional, replaceable, reliable, emotional, collectable, regrettable, functional, educational, remarkable

9 theatre (outdoors), nation, queue, station, phrase, drought, photo(graph), elephant, medal, plough

10 mouthguard, guesthouse, quarterfinal, guesswork, earthquake, whirlpool, photograph, wheelbarrow

TARGETING SPELLING 4 © PASCAL PRESS ISBN 9781925490220

5 Name the pictures. *(Hint: All are compound words)*

6 Write a synonym for each word using the first-letter clues.

stop	h______	sure	c______	chase	p______
width	br______	savage	f______	rich	w______
odd	st______	tall	h______	plank	b______
clap	ap______	robber	th______	final	l______

7 Answer the following questions.

What is a baby cow? ______

What is worn on the feet? ______

Who would scale a mountain? ______

What is a bird covered with? ______

What does ½ represent? ______

What do men carry their money in? ______

What structure spans a river? ______

Who is a person who steals things? ______

What is soccer played on? ______

Where do two walls meet? ______

8 Add a letter team to complete the words. Choose from e and ea.

I have a pair of **l**___**ther** boots. They are big, **r**___**d** and **h**___**vy**.

Dad will **m**___**sure** the **l**___**ngth** and **br**___**dth** of the room.

I took a deep **br**___**th** and dived **h**___**dfirst** into the pool.

We **f**___**d** the ducks with crusts of **br**___**d**.

W___**t w**___**ther** is expected **ah**___**d** of cold, **w**___**st** winds.

Syllables (closed)

The first syllable of a word often ends in a consonant sound. *Examples:* ***num**ber, **rub**bish, **mag**net*. The vowel is usually 'short'.

SEE & SAY

ticket	chicken	juggle	rumble
cricket	thicken	wriggle	tremble
rocket	written	shuffle	gentle
pocket	sudden	huddle	angle
bucket	kitchen	dazzle	ankle

1 Name the pictures.

THE 'e' RULE

When verbs end in le, drop the e before adding -ing and -ed. *Examples: trickle, trickl**ing**; tumble, tumbl**ing**; paddle, paddl**ed**; shuffle, shuffl**ed***

2 Add an ending to the word in bold to complete each sentence correctly.

twinkle Thousands of stars are ____________________ in the night sky.

tremble Jack ____________________ as the giant strode towards the beanstalk.

nibble The mice in the shed are ____________________ on grains of wheat.

sizzle Sausages are ____________________ in the hot frying pan.

rumble Overhead, the lightning flashed and thunder ____________________.

huddle The hens are ____________________ in a corner of the henhouse.

3 Write a letter in each square to spell the missing words. Here are the clues.

The bowler hit the bails off the ___.

I have fifty cents in my ___.

After rain, we like to splash in the ___.

Dad bought ___ to the final soccer game.

Tigers live in the thick, dark ___.

w						
p						
p						
t						
j						

TARGETING SPELLING 4 © PASCAL PRESS ISBN 9781925490220

4 Complete this table of rhyming words.

rumble	
m_______	h_______
t_______	gr_______
b_______	cr_______
f_______	st_______

MEMORY TRAINING

Read the words in each list two times. How many words can you remember? Write them in your notebook. Check and write your score here.

....

LOOK & LEARN

how during evening caught

5 Read the words then match them to their meanings. Use a dictionary to help you.

cricketer	1. a drinking glass 2. a gymnast (noun)
settler	a person who plays the game of cricket (noun)
muffler	a person who fishes with a hook and line (noun)
tumbler	common name for a mosquito larva (noun)
angler	a person who chooses to live in a new area or country (noun)
wriggler	a drinking fountain (noun)
bubbler	a warm scarf (noun)

6 Colour the pairs of words that make a compound word. Use a different colour for each pair.

saddle	blue	pocket	bumble	paddle	candle
boat	knife	stick	bag	bottle	bee

7 Write three sentences. Begin with the following phrases.

On long winter evenings, ______________________________

During the cricket match, ______________________________

In our kitchen, ______________________________

8 Colour the correct word in the brackets.

John will [snuffle shuffle] the cards and deal them out.

Dr Figg used a [bottle battle] to collect a [simple sample] of creek water.

As the clown [juggles jungles] the balls, he steps into a [paddle puddle].

The bird [raffled ruffled] its feathers and [settled saddled] on to its perch.

The [bungle bundle] of clothes was dirty and [wriggled wrinkled].

Syllables (open)

The first syllable of a word often ends in a vowel.
Examples: ***spider***, ***baby***, ***robot***
The vowel is 'long' (says its own name).

SEE & SAY

begin	**station**	**able**	**rifle**
moment	**siren**	**table**	**trifle**
ruby	**famous**	**cable**	**title**
bacon	**final**	**stable**	**bridle**
radar	**program**	**fable**	**bugle**

1 Add endings to complete the words in bold.

Take a few **moment**_____ to read the **begin**_____ paragraph.

All the horses have **final**_____ been **stable**_____ for the night.

The riders put their **saddle**_____ and **bridle**_____ in the tack room.

Soldier_____ with **rifle**_____ are **station**_____ on the **rooftop**_____.

Miss Prim is wearing a gold ring **stud**_____ with red **ruby**_____.

2 Add -ly to these words to form adverbs.

famous	famously	total	___________
final	___________	vibrant	___________
able	___________	secret	___________
recent	___________	stupid	___________
vocal	___________	silent	___________

LOOK & LEARN

sure post front kind

3 Write three sentences using these compound words: tablecloth, signpost, timetable.

____

____

____

____

____

____

TARGETING SPELLING 4 © PASCAL PRESS ISBN 9781925490220

4 Build the words you know. Say and write the words then match them to their meanings.

mo tor	motor	a picture taken with a camera (noun)
gi ant	____________	an engine (noun)
vi brate	____________	an insect like a grasshopper (noun)
ma jor	____________	huge; enormous (noun or adjective)
pho to	____________	move back and forth quickly; shake; tremble (verb)
lo cust	____________	greater in importance (noun or adjective)

5 Cross out (✗) the incorrect word in the brackets.

She wore a beautiful white [bridle bridal] gown.

I will [stable staple] the pages of my story together.

Read the [title tidal] of your poem to me, please.

[Solar Polar] energy comes from the sun.

Planes are tracked across the sky by [radio radar].

6 Add the missing vowels: a, e, i, o, u.

The **b__ker** is wearing an **__pron** over his **cl__thing**.

My **f__vourite** sporting **__vent** is the 100 **m__tre** sprint.

My **m__sic** exam will be held **l__ter** in **J__ly**.

Pl__to is a **t__ny**, **fr__zen** planet billions of **kilom__tres** away from Earth.

The **s__l__ist** sang into a **m__cr__ph__ne**.

7 Colour the pairs of words that are synonyms. Use a different colour for each pair.

tulip	student	human	pirate	baby	donate	lady
person	give	infant	flower	pupil	woman	robber

8 Use the letters in this word to make new words.

procrastinates

Score 1 point for each 3-letter word.
Score 3 points for each 4-letter word.
Score 5 points for each 5-letter word.

3-letter words ____

____

4-letter words ____

____

5-letter words ____

____

Words ending in y

Words that end in the letter y are **nouns**, **adjectives** or **verbs**. When you add a *common ending*, think about how to use the y rule.

country	story	apply	hurry
family	library	reply	carry
beauty	sturdy	rely	study
city	busy	deny	obey
monkey	dirty	bury	annoy

THE 'y' RULE

To write the plural form of **nouns** ending in y, follow these simple rules:
1 If the letter before the y is a vowel, just add -s. *Examples: boys, keys*
2 If the letter before the y is **not** a vowel, change y to i and add -es. *Example: baby, babies*

1 Write these nouns in plural form.

family	______	country	______	duty	______
monkey	______	library	______	chimney	______
city	______	donkey	______	story	______
valley	______	cherry	______	gully	______

When comparing **adjectives** ending in y, change y to i before adding -er or -est. *Example: happy, happier, happiest*
To form **adverbs**, change y to i before adding -ly. *Example: happy, happily*

2 Complete this table of adjectives and adverbs.

Add -er		Add -est		Add -ly	
sturdy	______	dirty	______	busy	______
dizzy	______	cosy	______	dainty	______
bumpy	______	cuddly	______	crazy	______
cloudy	______	funny	______	pretty	______
steady	______	happy	______	ordinary	______

LOOK & LEARN

saw ask orange lemon

TARGETING SPELLING 4 © PASCAL PRESS ISBN 9781925490220

To change the tense of **regular verbs** ending in **y**, follow these simple rules:

1 Add **-ing** to verbs ending in **y**. *Examples: playing, carrying*

2 If the letter before the **y** is a vowel, just add **-s** or **-ed**.
Example: plays, played

3 If the letter before the **y** is **not** a vowel, change **y** to **i** and add **-es** or **-ed**.
Example: try, tries, tried

Complete this table.

	Present tense		Past tense
cry	cries	crying	cried
obey			
reply			
annoy			
study			
carry			
bury			

Circle the correct word in the brackets.

I [saw seen] a dove last week, but I've never [saw seen] a hawk.

I haven't [did done] my homework yet, but Jillian [has have].

Jake [went gone] to the park, but Jay has [went gone] to the movies.

Did you [saw see] who [went gone] with John to the beach?

I [did done] my chores before I [went gone] out to play.

Colour the pairs of words that are synonyms. Use a different colour for each pair.

rely	duty	country	reply	story	annoy	frisky
nation	tale	depend	playful	irritate	task	answer

Here is a list of adjectives. Write a suitable noun beside each one.

busy ____________ annoying ____________

reliable ____________ beautiful ____________

sturdy ____________ studious ____________

silly ____________ merry ____________

obedient ____________ extraordinary ____________

Write a sentence about buried treasure.

____

____

Silent Letters: k, w

Words with 'silent letters' are very old. The **k** in ***knight*** and the **w** in ***write*** were once pronounced. They fell 'silent' because people found them hard to pronounce, but they became trapped in the spelling. Because what we *see* and what we *say* are different, we need to remember what they *look* like.

SEE & SAY

knob	know	write	wring
knot	knife	wrote	wrong
knit	knight	written	wrist
knock	kneel	answer	wreck
knuckle	knelt	sword	

1 Name the pictures.

2 Add an ending to the word in bold to complete each sentence correctly.

write The reporter is ________________ an article for the evening news.

knife Set the table with six ________________, forks and spoons, please.

wrong Tammy answered the question ________________.

knit Mum is ________________ me a warm scarf and beanie.

knot I ________________ the rope tightly around the post.

knob The young colt has long legs and ________________ knees.

LOOK & LEARN

clothes wash meant mighty

3 Join the word parts to make compound words.

knap	knob	knit	hood
wrist	out	pocket	fish
knee	sack	knight	pads
ship	watch	knee	knife
door	cap	door	wear
knock	wreck	sword	knocker

UNIT 20

4 Write words of opposite meaning and find them in the word search.

question	______________
right	______________
ugly	______________
clean	______________
shout	______________
last	______________
sooner	______________
worst	______________

t	c	l	r	f	s	e	g	q
s	g	n	o	r	w	l	t	d
j	o	g	d	y	h	o	p	n
b	e	a	u	t	i	f	u	l
e	n	n	o	r	s	i	g	a
s	d	s	l	i	p	r	k	t
t	u	w	c	d	e	s	i	e
m	b	e	t	y	r	t	j	r
o	e	r	n	v	u	p	a	x

5 Colour the correct word in the brackets.

I don't [no know] which [road rode] to follow to get to Tom's house.

The baker [needs kneads] the dough to make some [bred bread].

Sally [new knew] it was the [right write] [weigh way] to the zoo.

[Ring Wring] the water out of the wet [close clothes].

Benjamin [tide tied] his shoelaces in a [knot not].

6 Colour the pairs of words that are synonyms. Use a different colour for each pair. Use a dictionary to help you.

writhe	wren	wrath	wreathe	wrap	wrench	wreck
surround	twist	bird	enclose	squirm	ruin	anger

7 Match each word to its meaning by writing its number in the box. Use a dictionary to help you.

1 know-all 2 knob 3 knuckle 4 knick-knack
5 knoll 6 knack 7 knave 8 knowledge

	finger joint near the hand		a particular skill
	a rascal, rogue or scoundrel		a skite or boastful person
	learning		a handle for a door or drawer
	a pretty ornament		a rounded hill

How many words can you remember?

Go back and choose any *See and Say* list. Read through it twice, focusing on how the words look and sound. Write as many words as you can remember in your notebook. Check how many you have written correctly and enter your score here.

Silent Letters: b, t

Words with 'silent letters' are very old. The **b** in *climb* and *bomb*, and the **t** in *castle*, would have once been pronounced. Because these words are rather different when we *see* them and *say* them, we need to remember what they *look* like.

lamb	thumb	listen	whistle	castle
limb	crumb	glisten	thistle	rustle
comb	climb	fasten	nestle	
numb	debt	hasten	wrestle	
dumb	doubt			

1 Name the pictures.

2 Add an ending to the word in bold to complete each sentence correctly.

whistle A cold wind was ____________________ through the open doorway.

listen Dad always ____________________ to the morning news on the radio.

doubt It is ____________________ that it will rain today.

glisten Dew ____________________ on the grass in the morning sunshine.

comb Jane ____________________ back her hair and fastened it with a ribbon.

rustle Leaves are ____________________ in the soft autumn breeze.

-er is often added to **verbs** to show what some people and things do.
Examples: someone who *runs* is a *runner*; something that *washes* is a *washer*

3 Name the following people or things.

One who wrestles	____________	One who climbs	____________
One who listens	____________	One who whistles	____________
One who writes	____________	One who knits	____________
That which wrings	____________	That which knocks	____________
That which fastens	____________	That which wraps	____________

TARGETING SPELLING 4 © PASCAL PRESS ISBN 9781925490220

When endings are added to some words ending in a silent **b**, the **b** is usually sounded.
*Examples: crum**b**, crum**ble**; lim**b**, lim**ber**, lim**bo***

4 Place a letter in each box to spell the missing words.

The referee blew his ___ to stop the game.
Sarah is ___ her long blonde hair.
Kenny is ___ into his sleeping bag.
Sam can't repay his ___.
We ___ to the news on the radio last night.
The sheep and their new ___ are in the field.

w							
c							
n							
d							
l							
l							

LOOK & LEARN

through against true false

5 Join the word parts to read the compound words. Match them to their meanings.

ginger‿bread	a model of a castle built in sand usually by children
dumb‿bell	1. crest on head of rooster 2. a red-flowering garden plant
thistle‿down	small pieces of broken bread
bread‿crumbs	sweet food flavoured with ginger
sand‿castle	a hand-held weight used in training to strengthen muscles
cocks‿comb	light, feathery material that carries thistle seeds in the wind

6 Are these statements True or False?

You would fasten your coat with nails. ________
Arms and legs are human limbs. ________
You have a thumb on each foot. ________
It would be wise to wrestle a crocodile. ________
Fortress is a synonym for *castle*. ________
A breeze would make leaves rustle. ________
Ice and snow can numb your fingers. ________
A lamb is a baby goat. ________

7 Unscramble these baby animals. Begin with the letter in bold.

d**k**i ________	bma**l** ________	f**c**la ________	**c**bu ________
lao**f** ________	pp**p**yu ________	w**f**na ________	igtl**p**e ________

Letter Teams: oi, oy

The letter teams oi and oy work together in a word to make the sound oy, as heard in *oil* and *soil*, and *boy* and *toy*.
oi is usually in the middle of a word and oy is usually at the end.

SEE & SAY

spoil	voice	enjoy	loyal
hoist	choice	employ	royal
moist	point	annoy	oyster
avoid	appoint	destroy	

1 Add endings to the words in bold to complete the sentences correctly.

The **boy**____ in the team have **appoint**____ me as their captain.

I **moisten**____ a cloth and **wipe**____ the whiteboard.

The teacher is **annoy**____ because Joe has been **avoid**____ piano practice.

The **girl**____ have **join**____ a chess club and are **enjoy**____ playing.

Their **noise**____ game was **spoil**____ when it **start**____ to rain.

2 Colour the pairs of words that are synonyms. Use a different colour for each pair.

loyal	join	destroy	avoid	royal	annoy	moist
bother	dodge	damp	faithful	ruin	connect	regal

3 Colour the letter before the correct answer to reveal an annoying insect.

Milk will ___ if left in the sun.	D	soil	M	spoil
___ the flag to the top of the pole.	R	haul	O	hoist
Jimmy tried to ___ the mud puddles.	S	avoid	G	evade
You have a ___ between pasta and pizza.	A	choose	Q	choice
The children were ___ at Tilly's party.	U	joyful	F	joyless
Some snakes inject ___ through their fangs.	I	poison	L	person
I found a shiny silver ___ in the grass.	Y	corn	T	coin
Put the eggs in a pot and ___ them.	O	boil	S	broil

This insect is a ____________________.

LOOK & LEARN

animal money almost among

TARGETING SPELLING 4 © PASCAL PRESS ISBN 9781925490220

Join the syllables to read the words. Match them to their meanings. Use a dictionary to help you.

voy age	one of thousands of small, solid bodies that orbit the sun
an droid	extreme confusion; disorder
de coy	a long journey especially by sea
tur quoise	a robot that looks and moves like a human
as ter oid	something used to lure someone into danger or into a trap
tur moil	1. blue-green colour 2. mineral prized as a gemstone

Add a letter team to complete the words. Choose from oi and oy.

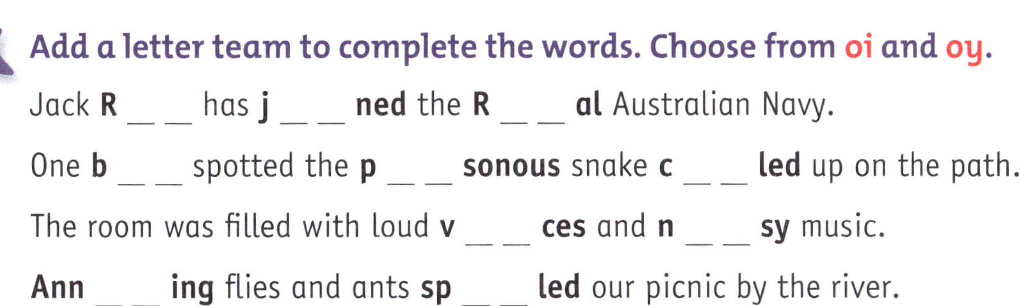

Jack **R** __ __ has **j** __ __ **ned** the **R** __ __ **al** Australian Navy.

One **b** __ __ spotted the **p** __ __ **sonous** snake **c** __ __ **led** up on the path.

The room was filled with loud **v** __ __ **ces** and **n** __ __ **sy** music.

Ann __ __ **ing** flies and ants **sp** __ __ **led** our picnic by the river.

My **empl** __ __ **er** has **app** __ __ **nted** me chief editor.

A **suffix** is a **syllable** attached to the end of a word to build a **noun**, an **adjective**, a **verb** or an **adverb**. *Examples: enjoyment* (noun), *enjoyable* (adjective), *moisten* (verb), *moistly* (adverb)

Build new words by adding suffixes. Write the words on the line.

royal + ty	____________	loyal + ty	____________
joy + ful + ly	____________	appoint + ment	____________
joy + ous + ly	____________	avoid + able	____________
point + er	____________	avoid + ance	____________
destroy + er	____________	employ + ment	____________

Use the letters in this word to make new words.

festival

Score 1 point for each 3-letter word.
Score 3 points for each 4-letter word.
Score 5 points for each 5-letter word.

3-letter words ________________________________

____

4-letter words ________________________________

____

5-letter words ________________________________

____

Letter Teams: air, are, ear

The letter teams **air** and **are** have the same sound **air**, as in ***hair*** and ***chair***, and ***care*** and ***share***. Sometimes **ear** shares this sound, as in the words ***wear*** and ***bear***.

SEE & SAY

pair	despair	bare	parent	wear
lair	dairy	square	prepare	bear
repair	fairy	scare	compare	pear
		scarce	declare	tear
				swear

1 **Write these nouns in their plural form. *(Remember the 'y' rule.)***

square ____________ fairy ____________ pair ____________ parent ____________ dairy ____________

LOOK & LEARN

pizza pasta steak salad

2 **Add endings to the words in bold to complete the sentences.**

prepare Dad is cooking steak and mum is ____________ a salad.

compare I am tall ____________ to my friend Jesse.

dairy Many farmers are involved in ____________ in rural Australia.

bare There was ____________ enough for the people to eat.

fair Everyone said they had been treated ____________.

dare The police carried out a ____________ sea rescue.

3 **Join the word parts to build new words.**

hair < y / less

fair < ly / ness

care < less / ful

____________ ____________ ____________

____________ ____________ ____________

4 **Use two of the new words above in sentences.**

____

____

TARGETING SPELLING 4 © PASCAL PRESS ISBN 9781925490220

5 Join the word parts to make compound words.

hair	house	soft	taker
bare	ware	care	way
ware	brush	down	crow
hard	case	stair	ware
stair	foot	scare	stairs

6 Colour the correct word in the brackets.

Larry grew up on a [quite quiet] [dairy diary] farm in Queensland.

Her head was [bear bare] and her [hare hair] shone gold in the sunshine.

We saw the distress [flair flare] in the dark [knight night] sky.

Tinker sprinkled [fairy ferry] dust on the [flour flower] in Gina's [hare hair].

We paid our [fair fare] and climbed the [stairs stares] into the bus.

Our [team teem] is known for its ball handling skills and [fare fair] play.

7 Complete this table of present and past tense verbs. *(*irregular verbs.)*

	Present tense		Past tense
repair	(he) repairs	(he is) repairing	(he) repaired
wear *			
compare			
tear *			
prepare			
stare			
swear *			

8 Write sentences to show the difference in meaning between 1. pair and pear and 2. bear and bare.

1 ______________________________

____

2 ______________________________

____

9 Complete this short quiz.

Name a rabbit-like animal. h__________

Where is milk produced? d__________

Who are your mother and father? p__________

What is a female horse? m__________

What must you pay to travel on a bus or train? f__________

Prefixes: a-, al-

A **prefix** is a syllable attached to the beginning of a word. The prefix **a-** is attached to many words and comes from an old English word meaning 'on', 'in', 'into', 'to' or 'towards'. *Example: **ashore** = on to the shore.* When **all** is placed at the beginning of a word, it is shortened to **al-**. *Example: all ways = **always***

SEE & SAY

ago	along	alive	always	almighty
again	aloud	alone	already	also
afraid	alert	amaze	alright	although
ahead	alike	amuse	almost	altogether

1 **Add the missing letters to complete the words. All begin with the prefix a- *('uh' sound).***

We walked **a**l _ _ _ the beach looking for shells.

The cat ran **a**w _ _ when the dog barked.

The teacher asked me to read my story **a**l _ _ _ to the class.

Many years **a**g _, Matthew Flinders sailed **a**r _ _ _ _ Australia.

I was too **a**fr _ _ _ to venture into the deep, dark forest.

You go **a**h _ _ _ and I'll follow you.

2 **Build the words you know by adding the prefix a- *(pronounced 'uh').***

wake	awake	way	______	loft	______
sleep	______	glow	______	lone	______
board	______	void	______	shamed	______
shore	______	float	______	part	______
blaze	______	far	______	ware	______

3 **Place a letter in each box to spell the missing words. Use the sentence clues. All words begin with the prefix a-.**

Clue	Boxes
The children walked ___ the street to the park.	a _ _ _ _
The bushranger was wanted – dead or ___.	a _ _ _ _
The horses galloped ___ the racetrack.	a _ _ _ _ _
Lift your hands ___ your head.	a _ _ _ _
This story is ___ knights and dragons.	a _ _ _ _
I made a mistake and had to do the sum ___.	a _ _ _ _

TARGETING SPELLING 4 © PASCAL PRESS ISBN 9781925490220

UNIT 24

Don't confuse **already** and **all ready**.
Already means before an expected time.
All ready means everything is prepared. *Examples:*
The cakes are ***all ready*** *to be eaten. =* ***All*** *the cakes are* ***ready*** *to be eaten.*
The cakes have ***already*** *been eaten. (It's all over. There are none left!)*
Other words that might be confused are **alright** and **all right**, **altogether** and **all together**.

4 Circle the correct wording in the brackets.

I [already   all ready] have my coat on, so I'm [already   all ready] for school.

The teacher said that my sums were [alright   all right].

My toys are [altogether   all together] in a box under my bed.

Cormac is [already   all ready] for bed, but his twin is [already   all ready] there.

Our sporting equipment cost us $50 [altogether   all together].

Is it [alright   all right] if we go to the pool [altogether   all together]?

5 Write the words from the word wheel. Begin with the prefix a-.

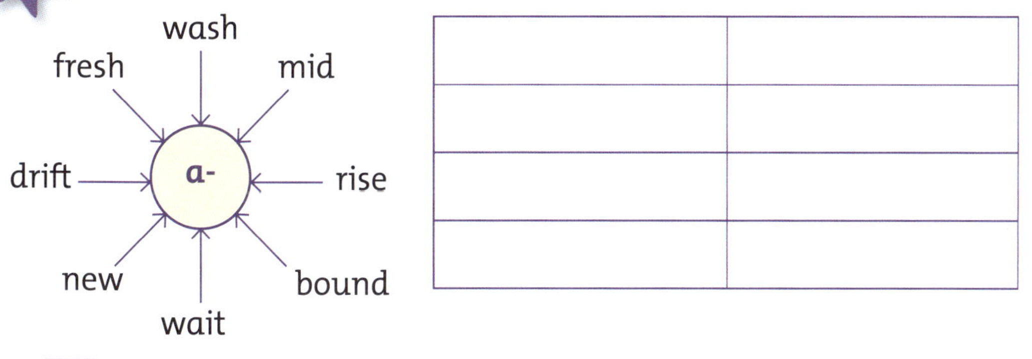

MEMORY TRAINING

Read the words in each list three times. How many words can you remember? Write them in your notebook. Check and write your score here.

....

LOOK & LEARN

another   whether   either   neither

6 Match the words to their meanings.

abroad	side by side
ajar	with the legs on either side of something
akimbo	away from your own country
abreast	partly open
astride	to turn away from; to prevent something from happening
avert	standing with hands on hips, elbows out

How many words can you remember?

Go back and choose any *See and Say* list. Read through it twice, focusing on how the words look and sound. Write as many words as you can remember in your notebook. Check how many you have written correctly and enter your score here.

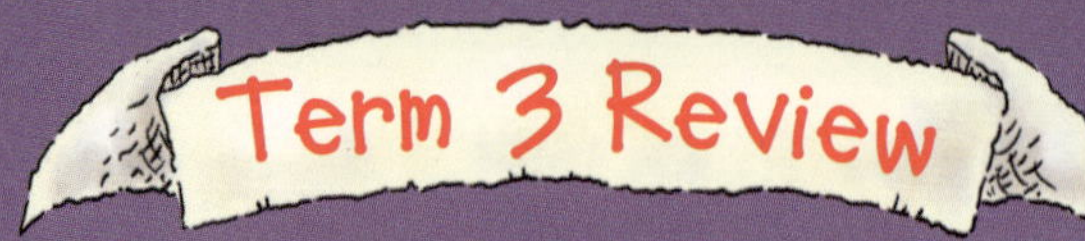

Term 3 Review

1 Name the pictures.

	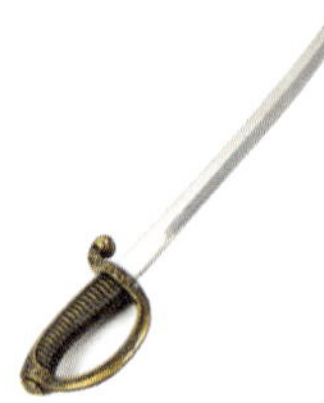			

2 Write these nouns in plural form.

lamb __________ ankle __________ family __________

knife __________ ruby __________ thistle __________

fairy __________ voice __________ monkey __________

city __________ story __________ crumb __________

3 Write antonyms *(words of opposite meaning)* for each of these words.

true __________ question __________ clean __________

rough __________ right __________ morning __________

behind __________ dead __________ city __________

least __________ back __________ end __________

4 Colour the correct word in the brackets.

In cold [whether weather] I wear warm [close clothes].

Did you [write right] this [tail tale] about a dragon and a [night knight]?

I combed my [hair hare] and put on my new [pare pair] of shoes.

The jockey put a [bridal bridle] and saddle on his [hoarse horse].

I don't [no know] the name of our city's [mare mayor].

5 Name the pictures. *(Hint: All are compound words)*

TARGETING SPELLING 4 © PASCAL PRESS ISBN 9781925490220

6 Complete this table of present and past tense verbs.

	Present tense		Past tense
enjoy	(she) enjoys	(she is) enjoying	(she) enjoyed
rely			
knit			
prepare			
write			
wear			
catch			

7 Write a synonym for each of the following words.

pail b__________ start b__________ depend r__________

night e__________ tale s__________ response a__________

forever a__________ hasten h__________ hear l__________

last f__________ lovely b__________ frightened s__________

8 Choose a suffix from the box to build a new word. Suffixes can be used more than once.

-ment -able -ly -ness -ful -er

gentle __________ beauty __________ bear __________

amaze __________ busy __________ employ __________

wrestle __________ avoid __________ amuse __________

enjoy __________ scarce __________ climb __________

9 Write a one-word answer to each of these questions.

What is a baby hen? __________

Where are cows milked? __________

What are cats, dogs, pigs and horses? __________

How many is a pair? __________

What shape has four equal sides? __________

What do you need to buy things? __________

Where is the stove in your house? __________

What does a rider place on a horse's head? __________

What do you turn to open a door? __________

Where would you go to catch a train? __________

Letter Teams: gu, qu

Words containing **gu** and **qu** date back thousands of years.
gu is pronounced as a 'hard' **g**, as in ***girl*** and ***goat***.
This means the **u** is not sounded. *Example:* ***guard*** *=* ***gard***
In English, **q** and **u** are always together as **qu**, which is usually pronounced as **kw**. *Examples:* ***queen, quick, quit***

SEE & SAY

guard	guitar	quick	query
guardian	guide	quit	queue
guess	guise	quite	squeal
guest	disguise	quiet	squash
guilty	penguin	quest	mosquito

1 **Write these nouns in their plural form.**

guest ______ query ______ guitar ______ guide ______ guess ______

2 **Add endings to the words in bold to complete the sentences.**

No one **guess**____ who was **disguise**____ as Batman.

The students **move**____ **quick**____ and **quiet**____ into the classroom.

Queue____ of people **gather**____ to see the fairy **penguin**____ **be**____ fed.

Bella **squeal**____ with delight when she heard the **strum**____ of **guitar**____.

Mosquito____ breed **quick**____ in the still water of **pond**____ and **puddle**____.

3 **Colour the pairs of words that are synonyms. Use a different colour for each pair.**

quit	guide	query	guest	guard	quiet	quest
search	visitor	silent	steer	question	leave	protect

4 **Complete this table of verbs.** ** Note the special past tense form of the verb.*

guard	guarding	guarded
queue		
guess		
disguise		

query		
guide		
squeal		
quit *		

LOOK & LEARN

daily monthly minute second

TARGETING SPELLING 4 © PASCAL PRESS ISBN 9781925490220

5 Read each of these qu words aloud and match them to their meanings. Use a dictionary to help you.

UNIT 25

quilt	satisfy (e.g. thirst); extinguish (e.g. fire) (verb)
quartet	group taking part in a shared activity (e.g. police, soldiers) (noun)
quaff	to spend or use wastefully (e.g. money, time, goods) (verb)
quiver	a light, warm bed cover (noun)
quench	a group of four people, especially of musicians or singers (noun)
quill	to drink down thirstily (verb)
squad	tremble or shake slightly (verb); case for holding arrows (noun)
squander	large feather; old-fashioned feather pen; spine of an echidna (noun)

6 Use the following words in sentences — 1. as a noun, 2. as a verb.

guess 1 ____________________

2 ____________________

guide 1 ____________________

2 ____________________

guard 1 ____________________

2 ____________________

7 Join the word parts to make compound words.

guest	quake	life	sand
mouth	book	guess	guard
guide	house	quick	final
earth	guard	quarter	work

WORD TRAPS

Don't confuse **quite** (adverb) and **quiet** (adjective).
*Examples: I arrived at school **quite** early. I have been **quite** busy today. The students were **quiet** and well-behaved. Jane is a shy and **quiet** child.*
Add **-ly** to **quiet** to form the adverb. *Example: Jane spoke **quietly**.*

8 Complete the sentences correctly. Choose from quite and quiet.

The forest grew __________ and dark, and I began to feel __________ afraid.

I couldn't __________ see over the wall because it was __________ high.

I was __________ pleased that the horse I rode was __________ and gentle.

The night was __________ and the air was still __________ warm.

Ella spoke in a __________ voice and it was __________ hard to hear her.

Word Endings: -el, -al

-el, -al and -le share the same sound l as in *camel*, *final* and *little*. Because words with these endings sound the same, you need to remember what the words *look* like.

SEE & SAY

camel	tunnel	oval	coral
level	pummel	rival	local
label	gravel	feral	plural
fuel	model	final	medal
cruel	angel	global	usual

1 Write these nouns in their plural form.

camel ____________ medal ____________ model ____________ label ____________ angel ____________

RULE When a verb ends in -el, double the l before adding -ing or -ed. *Examples: cancel, cancelling, cancelled; fuel, fuelling, fuelled; rebel, rebelling, rebelled*

2 Add an ending to the word in bold to complete each sentence correctly.

label I have ____________ my school bag and all my school books.

snorkel The tourists are ____________ in the warm tropical waters.

tunnel Trains travel under the city through huge, wide ____________.

model Sarah-Jane is ____________ the latest swimwear.

final The hikers ____________ reached the mountain top.

3 Add -ly to these words to form adverbs.

local ____________	total ____________	mental ____________
visual ____________	normal ____________	oral ____________
usual ____________	physical ____________	legal ____________
annual ____________	manual ____________	magical ____________

4 Name the pictures. *(Hint: All end in -el)*

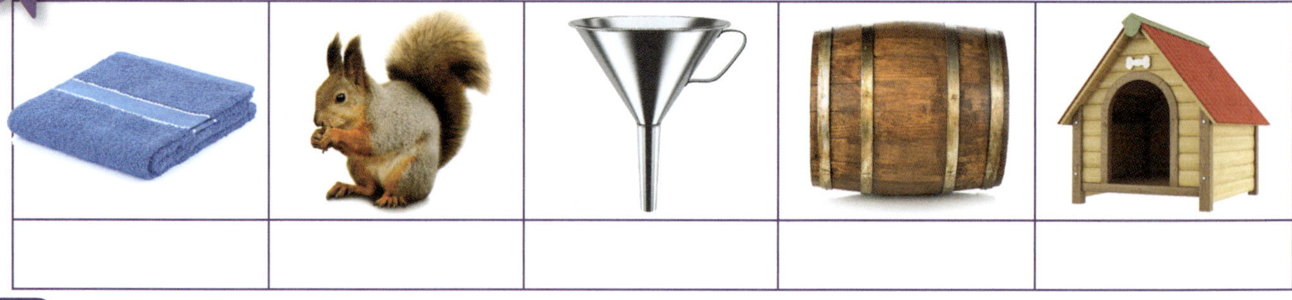

TARGETING SPELLING 4 © PASCAL PRESS ISBN 9781925490220

5 Here are more adjectives to add to your word bank. Join the syllables to say the words and match them to their meanings. Use a dictionary to help you.

ru ral	causing death; deadly
vo cal	concerning the spine or backbone
fa tal	necessary for life; essential; very important
pe nal	careful not to waste anything; thrifty
spi nal	relating to the country, country life or country people; rustic
vi tal	having to do with the voice
fru gal	of or involving punishment

LOOK & LEARN

first third nowhere anywhere

Some **pronouns** refer to people and things in a general way.
Examples: ***any****body,* ***some****one,* ***no****thing*
Adverbs also can refer to events in a general way.
Examples: ***any****how,* ***some****time,* ***no****where*

6 Read these words. Learn to spell them correctly, as you will write them often.

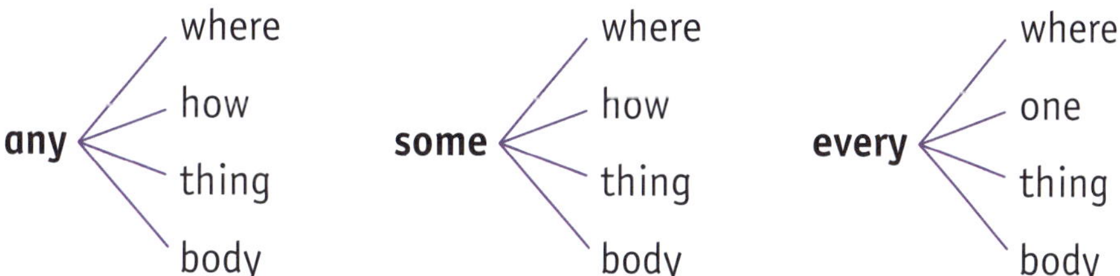

7 Add the correct letters to complete the words in bold. Choose from -el and -al.

When we **trav**___, we stay in **hot**___**s** or **mot**___**s**.

I am reading an interesting **historic**___ **nov**___ about Australia.

Improve your **physic**___ fitness with a sand-filled **pumm**___ ball.

Larry won a **med**___ for the **fin**___ race at the sports **carniv**___.

Some underwater **cor**___**s** look like the bright **pet**___**s** of flowers.

8 Write sentences to show how the word quarrel can be used 1. as a noun and 2. as a verb.

1 ____

2 ____

WORD TRAPS

Don't confuse **angle** and **angel**.
Think of an *angel* as having **gel** in her hair — an**gel**.
Don't confuse **naval** and **navel**. *Naval* is about the navy.
Navel is your belly button!

Letter Teams: ough

Words containing **ough** do **not** always have the same sound pattern. It is important to learn what these words *look* like.

SEE & SAY

ort		ŏff	ŭff	ō	(c)ow
ought	thought	cough	rough	dough	bough
bought	sought	trough	tough	though	plough
brought	fought		enough	although	drought

1 **Add endings to the words in bold to complete the sentences.**

The farmer **plough**____ his fields, ready for **plant**____.

Although Ashram is **cough**____, he **do**____ not have a cold.

You **real**____ must not treat your pet **animal**____ **rough**____.

Carly is a kind and **thought**____ person with excellent **manner**____.

I haven't seen Mr Tan **late**____ even though he **live**____ next door.

Colour the pairs of words that are synonyms. Use a different colour for each pair.

bough	drought	bought	trough	tough	enough	rough
purchased	plenty	bumpy	branch	famine	strong	trench

Though and **although** are **conjunctions** that join a **subordinate clause** to a **main clause**.
Examples: ***Although I looked everywhere,*** *I couldn't find my ball.*
The Earth is spinning rapidly, ***though you can't feel it moving.***

really
lately
finish
until

Add a main clause to these sentences.

Although it was past her bedtime, ______________________________

______________________________, though the sun had not yet risen.

Although it is raining, ______________________________

4 **Write these irregular verbs in past tense.**

Today I ...	Yesterday I ...	Today I ...	Yesterday I ...
fight	fought	teach	
buy		catch	
seek		draw	
think		swim	
bring		keep	

TARGETING SPELLING 4 © PASCAL PRESS ISBN 9781925490220

Don't confuse **though** and **through**.
Though is a **conjunction** introducing a **subordinate clause**.
Through is a **preposition** introducing a **phrase**.
*Examples: The bus didn't come, **though** I waited for ages.*
*I walked under a bridge, across a street and **through** a park.*

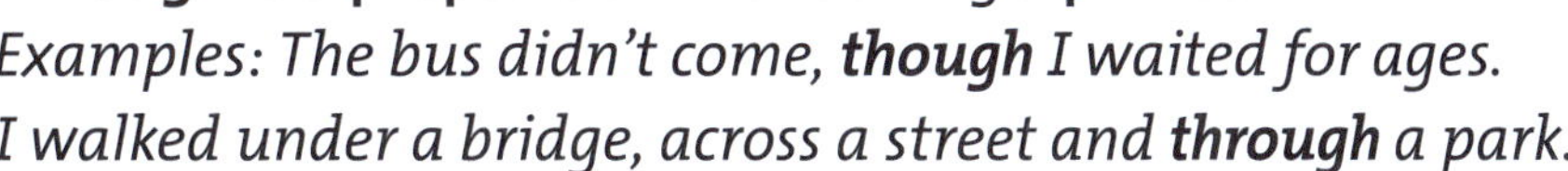

5 Colour the correct wording in the brackets.

The battle had [all ready already] been [fort fought] and [one won].
A sun [bare bear] sat nibbling berries on the [bough bow] of a tree.
We travelled by [plain plane] all [though through] the long, dark night.
A female [deer dear] is a [dough doe] and a female horse is a [mayor mare].
Dad says the new [pear pair] of jeans I [brought bought] are [quiet quite] nice.

6 Colour the letter before the correct response to reveal the answer to the question.

I don't have _______ money to buy a Lego house.	S	some	T	enough
In times of _______, farmers feed hay to their cattle.	H	drought	I	tough
Pam _______ her kitten to school in a basket.	A	bought	E	brought
The cows are drinking at the water _______.	N	bottle	S	trough
Blake _______ he would get all his sums right.	A	thought	R	think
I'll stay here _______ 4 o 'clock to finish my work.	U	until	P	unless
I could hear a cockatoo _______ I couldn't see it.	T	through	R	though
The hiker _______ shelter from the heavy rain.	U	sought	I	seek
The road _______ the mountains was narrow and rough.	E	threw	S	through

Which dinosaur knew the most words? ______________________.

7 Use the letters in this word to make new words.

thoroughfares

Score 1 point for each 3-letter word.
Score 3 points for each 4-letter word.
Score 5 points for each 5-letter word.

3-letter words ______________________________

____

4-letter words ______________________________

____

5-letter words ______________________________

____

Letter Teams: th, wh, ph

th is either **voiced** (*this, that, whether*) or **unvoiced** (*think, thumb, tooth*).
wh is a breathy sound like blowing out a candle (***w-hen, w-hat, w-here***).
Words containing **ph** are very old, with **ph** pronounced as **f** (***photo, phone***).

SEE & SAY

throb	whine	photo
thrust	whinge	phrase
throng	whimper	nephew
theatre	whether	elephant
thorough	whiff	graph
myth	whisk	triumph

1 Add endings to the words in bold to complete the sentences.

throb We heard the ____________________ sound of a helicopter overhead.

whisk My cat has long black ____________________.

triumph The winning team marched ____________________ around the field.

photo Mum likes to take ____________________ of old stone buildings.

whimper I could hear a puppy ____________________ outside my door.

throng Hundreds of people ____________________ to the football stadium.

2 Complete the table of present and past tense verbs.

	Present tense	Past tense
throb		
whine		
throw		
whinge		
think		
whimper		

Some verbs have an irregular past tense.
do → did
see → saw

3 Colour the pairs of words that are synonyms. Use a different colour for each pair.

throng	photo	myth	whiff	thrust	whinge	thorough
image	complain	puff	push	complete	legend	crowd

TARGETING SPELLING 4 © PASCAL PRESS ISBN 9781925490220

4 Join the word parts to make compound words.

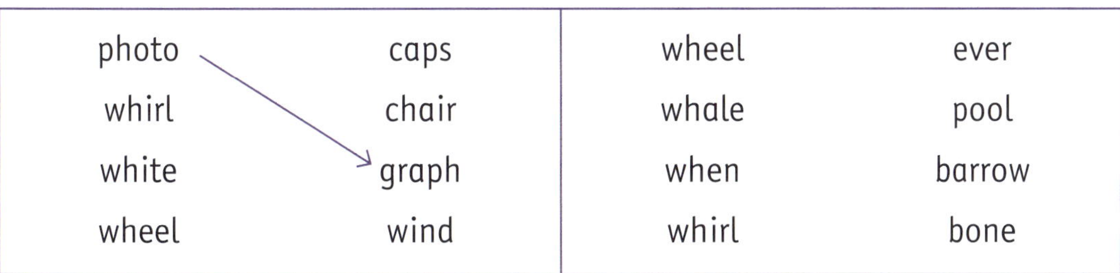

photo	caps	wheel	ever
whirl	chair	whale	pool
white	graph	when	barrow
wheel	wind	whirl	bone

LOOK & LEARN

hello goodbye usually youth

5 Join the syllables to write the words then match them to their meanings.

dol phin	dolphin	a large, long snake that wraps around its prey
or phan	____________	a mammal that lives in the sea
ty phoon	____________	captivate or enchant
whit tle	____________	the sound made by a horse
whin ny	____________	a child without parents
py thon	____________	a tropical cyclone or hurricane
en thrall	____________	to shape a piece of wood with a sharp knife

Don't confuse symphony and sympathy.
A **symphony** is a musical work. **Sympathy** is a feeling shared with someone, especially when they are sad.

6 Complete these words using th, ph or wh.

____ump	____oto	____ite	____ing
al____abet	____ese	____rase	____ole
____isker	____irsty	____em	ele____ant
____row	____ale	____one	____isper
hy____en	____rough	____eel	py____on

Here are some important little words we use every day. They all begin with wh-. Look at them carefully and learn to spell them correctly every time.

what when where why while who whose

How many words can you remember?

Go back and choose any *See and Say* list. Read through it twice, focusing on how the words look and sound. Write as many words as you can remember in your notebook. Check how many you have written correctly and enter your score here.

Prefixes: up-, down-

up- and **down-** are placed before many words to show whether something is going up or going down. Many antonyms are formed by adding **up-** and **down-**. *Examples:* ***up****stairs,* ***down****stairs;* ***up****hill,* ***down****hill.* Some words have only one direction. *Examples:* ***up****date,* ***up****-tempo;* ***down****hearted,* ***down****fall*

SEE & SAY

upstairs	**up**roar	**down**hill	**down**grade
upstream	**up**date	**down**hearted	**down**town
upstage	**up**grade	**down**pour	**down**stairs
upright	**up**turn	**down**pipe	**down**stream
uproot	**up**ward	**down**fall	**down**wards

You will already know many of the base words.

1 Add an ending to the word in bold to complete each sentence correctly.

update Dad has recently ____________________ our television set.

download I have ____________________ the information I need from the web.

uproot Trees were ____________________ in the violent storm.

uplift His story of hardship and survival was very ____________________.

downplay Jackson ____________________ his amazing record-breaking swim.

2 The following words can only be prefixed by either **up-** or **down-**. Add the correct one.

________play	________standing	________end	________pour
________hold	________on	________cast	________surge
________time	________fall	________set	________slide
________root	________rising	________trodden	________coming

3 Add **up-** and **down-** to the following words.

	up-	down-
river		
load		
side		
wind		
beat		
size		
swing		
stage		

TARGETING SPELLING 4 © PASCAL PRESS ISBN 9781925490220

LOOK & LEARN

happen suddenly move prove

UNIT 29

4 Complete the broken words in these sentences. They begin with up- or down-.

Cameron ran **d**________**st**________ and out through the back door.

It was hard work riding **u**_____**h**________ on my push bike.

The boat broke its moorings and floated away **d**________**st**________.

Poor Tom! He **u**_____**e**________**ed** his paint pot all over his work.

I will **d**________**l**________ some information about coral from the internet.

The local council will **u**_____**gr**________ Banks Street and include a bike lane.

The heavy **d**________**p**________ caused flash flooding in the city.

The teenagers went **d**________**t**________ to the shopping arcade.

in- and out- are two other prefixes that can be attached to words to show direction. Many **antonyms** are formed by adding in- and out-. *Example: **in**side, **out**side*

5 Write antonyms for these words by adding in- or out-.

indoors	outdoors	outbox	________
inside	________	output	________
inbound	________	outflow	________
infield	________	outgoing	________
inboard	________	outlet	________

6 Colour the correct word in the brackets.

There has been an [up down] surge in the cost of petrol.

Nancy was very [up down] set when she couldn't find her kitten.

The teacher said we all deserved some [up down] time.

We are very excited about the [up down] coming school concert.

Water rushed through the [up down] pipe and into the gutter.

7 Use the letters in this word to make new words.

d o w n s t r e a m

Score 1 point for each 3-letter word.
Score 3 points for each 4-letter word.
Score 5 points for each 5-letter word.

3-letter words ________________________

4-letter words ________________________

____

5-letter words ________________________

Prefixes: over-, under-

over- and **under-** are placed before many words to show whether something is above something or below something.
Examples: ***over**head*, ***over**pass*; ***under**ground*, ***under**line*
over- and **under-** are also used to give a sense of 'more' or 'less'.
Examples: ***over**cooked*, ***over**eat*; ***under**paid*, ***under**weight*

SEE & SAY

overhear	**over**joyed	**under**arm	**under**tow
overnight	**over**grown	**under**clothes	**under**line
overtake	**over**look	**under**wear	**under**pass
overturn	**over**board	**under**ground	**under**take
overseas	**over**weight	**under**water	**under**weight

You will already know many of the base words.

1 Choose a word from the *See and Say* list to complete the sentences.

Use a red pencil to ____________________ all the important words.

The sailor threw the anchor ____________________.

I can hold my breath and stay ____________________ for two minutes.

Any fish that are ____________________ must be returned to the sea.

We are going ____________________ for a six-month holiday.

The chimney had fallen and the garden was ____________________ with weeds.

2 Write the words from the word wheels.

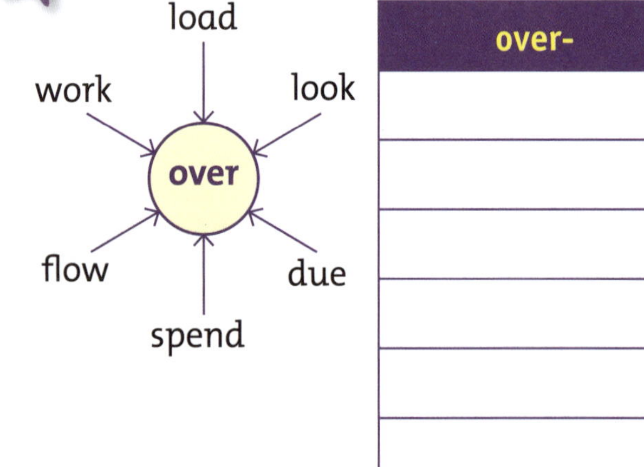

over-	under-

3 Write antonyms beginning with under-.

overrate	____________________	**over**cooked	____________________
overpaid	____________________	**over**lay	____________________
overripe	____________________	**over**achieve	____________________
overpriced	____________________	**over**populated	____________________

empty hungry they're couldn't

Add endings to the words in bold. *(Remember the spelling rules.)*

I was quickly **overtake**_____ by Jesse in the final foot race.

The tourists stood on a bridge **overlook**_____ the great waterfall.

The little boat **overturn**_____ in the choppy seas.

The students are **undertake**_____ their biggest project ever.

The gutters **overflow**_____ and water spilled into the street.

A patient is **undergo**_____ surgery in the operating theatre.

5 Colour the correct word in each pair.

We were over/under joyed when we saw an eagle soaring over/under head.

On very cold days, I wear a warm woollen over/under coat.

A surfer was caught in an over/under current and had to be rescued.

Over/Under night, the sky will be over/under cast with periods of rain.

In cricket, balls are bowled over/under arm.

Over/Under water diving is our family's favourite pastime.

6 Read these over- and under- words. Match them to their meanings.

overbalance	a strong current below the surface of the waves
overwrought	to erode or dig under the earth's surface causing it to weaken
overrule	to jut out over something
overhang	to topple over
understorey	working in secret
undermine	extremely excited or agitated
undertow	the plants growing beneath the canopy of a forest
undercover	to reject or decide against someone's ideas

7 Write two sentences. Use the words overboard and underground.

1 ____

____

2 ____

____

Prefixes: re-, de-

The prefixes **re-** and **de-** come to us from the old language of Latin. They are added to base words to change their meaning, like this:
re- = *again* or *back* (***re****build = build again;* ***re****pay = pay back)*
de- = *from, down, away, opposite* (***de****part = to part from;* ***de****press = to press down).*
Many base words also come from Latin, for example: ***scandere*** = *climb* (***de****scend = to climb down);* ***flectare*** = *bend* (***re****flect = to bend back)*

SEE & SAY

return	**regret**	**delete**	**defend**
remark	**repeat**	**describe**	**deserve**
remove	**recover**	**depart**	**demolish**
reflect	**rebuild**	**depend**	**deliver**
reduce	**replace**	**descend**	**detour**

1 Complete this table of verbs. *(Remember the spelling rules.)*

	Add -ing	Add -ed
recover		
remove		
reflect		
regret		

	Add -ing	Add -ed
depend		
delete		
descend		
describe		

2 Build the words you know by adding prefixes.

Add re-		Add de-	
_____group	_____tail	_____rail	_____light
_____tell	_____play	_____bate	_____tail
_____port	_____form	_____lay	_____brief
_____lay	_____verse	_____fuse	_____cay
_____view	_____ply	_____clare	_____port

3 Build the words you know by adding suffixes. *(Note the 'e' rule.)*

depart + ure ____________	recover + y ____________
replace + ment ____________	remove + al ____________
remove + able ____________	defend + able ____________
regret(t) + able ____________	delete + ion ____________

TARGETING SPELLING 4 © PASCAL PRESS ISBN 9781925490220

LOOK & LEARN

type past wasn't weren't

Match these verbs to their meanings. Use a dictionary to help you.

recover	to continue; to take up again after a pause
deplete	to prevent or advise against doing something
deter	to invent or plan something
deny	to get better after an illness; to find something that was lost
resume	to drive back; to keep something away (e.g. mosquitoes)
revert	to use most of something; to reduce the amount greatly
devise	to say something is not true; refuse (e.g. permission)
repel	to go back to a former habit, belief, practice or condition

Colour the correct word in each pair.

The teacher said we should revise / devise our work without relay / delay.

One detail / retail store has greatly reduced / deduced the price of many items.

Mr Argus said my deport / report on endangered animals deserved / reserved top marks.

Though I'm trying to reduce / deduce my weight, I can't desist / resist chocolate.

Defer / Refer the matter to the police, so they can retain / detain the culprit.

Circle the two spelling mistakes in each sentence. Write them correctly underneath.

We had to make a deter while the road was being repared.

________________ ________________

The fisherman wasnt able to recuver his lost crab pots.

________________ ________________

I regreted my decision to desend the mountain at night.

________________ ________________

The price of many tipes of cars has been reduest.

________________ ________________

After the storm past over the city, many houses had to be rebilt. ________ ________

Unscramble these modes of transport. Start with the letter in bold.

r**c**a ________	su**b** ________	to**b**a ________	**t**inar ________
eik**b** ________	r**t**kuc ________	rry**f**e ________	an**p**el ________

Suffixes: -ion

The Latin suffix **-ion** is attached to the end of a word to form a **noun**. When added to a word ending in **t** or **te**, it becomes **-tion** (the **e** is dropped). *Examples: elect, elec**tion**; illustrate, illustra**tion***

SEE & SAY

mention	station	relation	education
action	nation	collection	expedition
fraction	fiction	correction	explanation
lotion	function	invitation	completion
motion	option	illustration	competition

1 **Complete this short quiz. Choose your answers from the *See and Say* list.**

a drawing to go with a story ____________________

a country and all its people ____________________

a choice ____________________

the place to go to catch a train ____________________

a part of something, e.g. ½, ¼ ____________________

something soothing to rub on the skin ____________________

a group of things gathered together ____________________

a journey made for a special reason ____________________

a made-up story ____________________

someone who is part of a family group e.g. cousin ____________________

RULE

When a noun ends in **-ion**, add **-s** to write it in its plural form.
*Examples: nation**s**, action**s***
Not all nouns ending in **-ion** have a plural form. *Examples: educa**tion**, fic**tion***
If used as the **subject** of a sentence, such words are followed by a **singular verb**.

2 **Change these verbs to nouns by adding -ion. *(Remember to drop the e.)***

react	____________________	populate	____________________
create	____________________	invent	____________________
prevent	____________________	operate	____________________
exhaust	____________________	celebrate	____________________
delete	____________________	locate	____________________
reflect	____________________	subtract	____________________

LOOK & LEARN

loose tie fasten tight

TARGETING SPELLING 4 © PASCAL PRESS ISBN 9781925490220

UNIT 32

someone

3 Read these nouns. Match them to their meanings.

caution	one printing of a book, magazine or newspaper
portion	alertness and carefulness (noun); to give a warning to (verb)
edition	or something that is different from all the others
caption	a title or an explanation for a picture or illustration
intention	a firm plan or purpose
exception	a part or a share of something

4 Build adjectives by adding -al to these nouns.

exception	__________	education	__________
option	__________	fiction	__________
intention	__________	function	__________
nation	__________	emotion	__________
addition	__________	tradition	__________

Some words ending in -ion can be both a **noun** and a **verb**.
Examples: caution, mention, function, section, station, question

5 Write a syllable in each box to spell the missing words, e.g. | op | er | a | tion |

Students go to school to receive an ______.

I won $20 in a colouring-in ______.

Sandy sent me an ______ to her birthday party.

We waited at the ______ for the six o'clock train.

The book I am reading has colourful ______.

The ______ of the city has grown to a million people.

6 Complete this table of verbs.

	Add -s	Add -ing	Add -ed
loosen			
fasten			
tighten			
tie			

How many words can you remember?

Go back and choose any *See and Say* list. Read through it twice, focusing on how the words look and sound. Write as many words as you can remember in your notebook. Check how many you have written correctly and enter your score here.

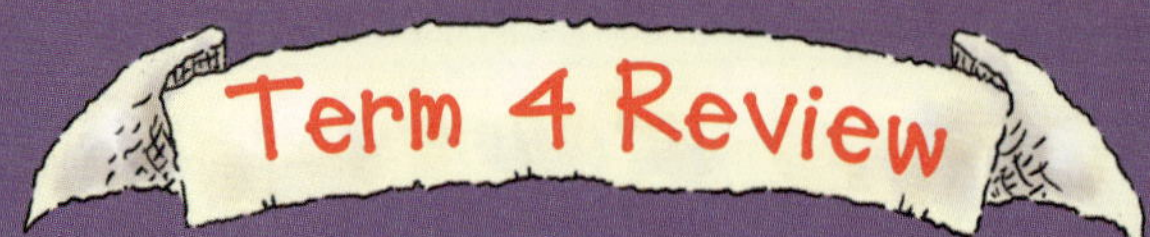

1 **Name the pictures.**

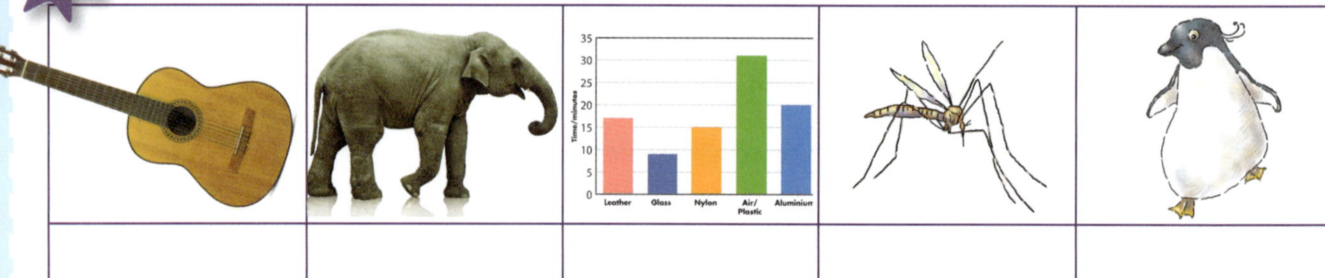

2 **Write these nouns in plural form.**

myth	________	model	________	option	________
guess	________	disguise	________	query	________
question	________	fraction	________	detour	________
bough	________	throng	________	relation	________

3 **Write antonyms for these words.**

underarm	________	upgrade	________	loud	________
loose	________	overweight	________	full	________
last	________	innocent	________	fact	________
usual	________	downstream	________	niece	________

4 **Colour the correct word in the brackets.**

I am [quiet quite] happy with the new shoes Mum [brought bought] for me.

I don't know [weather whether] to leave or wait till the storm has [past passed].

The hotel [guest guess] [brought bought] his luggage into the lobby.

Sharna was a [quite quiet] girl with gold hair and the face of an [angle angel].

The [whether weather] has been [quiet quite] cloudy today.

I'm not at all sleepy [through though] it is [passed past] my bedtime.

5 **Complete this table of present and past tense verbs.**

	Add -s	Add -ing	Add -ed
level			
query			
deserve			
throb			
regret			
guide			

TARGETING SPELLING 4 © PASCAL PRESS ISBN 9781925490220

6 Complete the words by adding an ending. Choose from -el, -al or -le.

We heard the train **whist**____ as it entered the **tunn**____.

The **catt**____ trucks bumped over the rough **grav**____ road.

A **cam**____ is an **unusu**____ **anim**____ with a hump on its back.

We like to **snork**____ over the **cor**____ reefs.

Peop____ are worried about **fer**____ **anim**____**s** in their **loc**____ area.

In the **fin**____ race, we had to run twice around the **ov**____.

7 Add a prefix to complete the words. Choose from up-, down-, over- or under-.

The castle grounds were ________**grown** with weeds and wildflowers.

The rider reached high speeds on the ________**hill** run to the finish line.

The diver rolled ________**board** and swam ________**water** for ten minutes.

Trees were ________**rooted** and cars were ________**turned** in the tornado.

Cricketers bowl ________**arm**. Softball players pitch ________**arm**.

8 Add -al or -able to build adjectives.

depend ____________________

fiction ____________________

remove ____________________

option ____________________

replace ____________________

rely ____________________

emotion ____________________

collect ____________________

regret ____________________

function ____________________

education ____________________

remark ____________________

9 Write a one-word answer to each of these questions.

Where are large concerts held? ____________________

What is a country and all its people? ____________________

What is a line of people waiting their turn? ____________________

Where do people go to catch a train? ____________________

What is a group of words without a verb? ____________________

What is a very long period of dry weather? ____________________

What is taken by a camera? ____________________

What is the world's largest land animal? ____________________

What is presented to an Olympic Games winner? ____________________

What implement does a farmer use to turn over the soil? ____________________

10 Colour the pairs of words that make a compound word. Use a different colour for each pair.

mouth	guest	quarter	guess	earth	whirl	photo	wheel
quake	work	pool	barrow	final	house	guard	graph

The Top 3 Spelling Rules

Rules	How to apply the rule	Examples
1 Doubling rule	When there is only ONE consonant after a short vowel, **double** that consonant before you add *-ing*, *-ed*, *-y*, *-er* or *-est*.	hop hopping skip skipped fun funny big bigger biggest
	If there are already TWO consonants after the short vowel, just add an ending.	jump jumping pack packed dust dusty rich richer richest
2 The *e* rule	When a word ends in ***e***, drop the ***e*** before adding an ending that begins with a vowel or ***y***.	ride riding shine shiny prickle prickly
	Do NOT drop the ***e*** when adding ***-ly*** (or any suffix beginning with a consonant).	safe safely safety use useful useless
3 The *y* rule	When a noun ends in ***y***, follow these simple rules to write its plural: 1 If the letter before the ***y*** is a vowel, just add ***-s***. 2 If the letter before the ***y*** is NOT a vowel, change ***y*** to ***i*** and add ***-es***.	boys days monkeys baby babies lady ladies
	When a regular verb ends in ***y***, follow these simple rules to write it in present or past tense: 1 Just add ***-ing***. 2 If the letter before the ***y*** is a vowel, just add ***-s*** or ***-ed***. 3 If the letter before the ***y*** is NOT a vowel, change ***y*** to ***i*** and add ***-es*** or ***-ed***.	fly flying carry carrying play plays played enjoy enjoys enjoyed cry cries cried hurry hurries hurried
	When an adjective ends in ***y***, change ***y*** to ***i*** and add ***-er*** or ***-est*** (comparing) and ***-ly*** (adverbs of manner).	happier happiest happily lazier laziest lazily

Common Endings

Ending	Purpose	Examples	Rule
-s	Add ***-s*** to MOST nouns to write them in plural form. Add ***-s*** to present tense verbs when the subject is *'he'*, *'she'* or *'it'*.	dogs apples toys hats runs plays rains growls eats stares swims	
-es	Add ***-es*** to nouns and verbs that end in ***s***, ***ss***, ***z***, ***zz***, ***x***, ***sh***, ***ch***.	buses dishes foxes tosses buzzes itches	
-ing	Add ***-ing*** to verbs to make present participles.	going jumping crying hopping rid~~e~~ing	1, 2, 3
-ed	Add ***-ed*** to *regular* verbs to make past participles.	planted clapped played carried baked	1, 2, 3
-y	Add ***-y*** to form adjectives.	bumpy funny ston~~e~~y	1, 2
-er -est	Add ***-er*** or ***-est*** to show how adjectives and adverbs compare.	taller tallest bigger biggest busier busiest faster fastest	1, 2, 3
-ly	Add ***-ly*** to form adverbs of manner.	quickly lately noisily	2, 3